THE NEW
MASTER
YOUR
MONEY

A STEP-BY-STEP
PLAN FOR GAINING
AND ENJOYING
FINANCIAL FREEDOM

RON BLUE

WITH JEREMY WHITE

FOREWORD BY CHARLES R. SWINDOLL

MOODY PUBLISHERS
CHICAGO

All Scripture quotations, unless otherwise indicated, are taken from the *New King James Version.* Copyright © 1982 by Thomas Nelson, Inc. Used by permission. All rights reserved.

Scripture quotations marked NIV are taken from the *Holy Bible, New International Version**. NIV* Copyright © 1973, 1978, 1984 by the International Bible Society. Used by permission of Zondervan Publishing House. All rights reserved.

Published in association with the literary agency of Wolgemuth and Associates.

Holmes and Rahe chart on page 75–76 is reprinted by permission from *Journal of Psychosomatic Research,* T. H. Holmes and R. H. Rahe, "The Social Readjustment Rating Scale," v. 11, 1967, Pergamon Press.

Material on estate planning on page 218–229 is taken from *Splitting Heirs* © 2004 by Ron Blue. Published by Northfield, an imprint of Moody Publishers. Used by permission.

ISBN 0-7394-4573-1

Printed in the United States of America

CONTENTS

FOREWORD

I am no authority when it comes to money matters.

Because this is true I have needed to seek help from those who are. While I may not know much about the subject of finances, I am a fairly good judge of character traits like integrity, authenticity, spiritual sensitivity, biblical awareness, and genuine humility. When someone possesses these qualities in addition to professional competence in the sometimes complicated world of finance, I sit up and take notice, . . . which explains why Ron Blue and I have cultivated such a close friendship.

For quite some time I have admired his convictions, sought his counsel, listened to his advice, and put his principles to the test. I have yet to regret one moment of that process. He is a rare find in this day of rapid-fire, shoot-from-the-hip high rollers who talk the language but fail to pattern their lives according to scriptural standards. This is what I appreciate most about Ron—he models his message. Quietly, graciously, thoroughly, the man represents what he presents. Because he keeps it so simple, even I can understand it! And that, my friend, is a minor miracle.

Almost twenty years ago I suggested to Ron that he dedicate himself to publishing his material. It seemed a shame that such resourceful and helpful information be available to so few. I am delighted he took up the challenge and disciplined himself to putting his valuable knowledge and techniques into print.

His book addresses numerous subjects that are of interest to all of us: developing a biblical philosophy of personal finances, getting (and staying) out of debt, establishing financial goals, achieving financial independence, overcoming consumptive spending, exposing many tax-planning myths, and cultivating the joy of generous giving as God designed for His people—to name only a few. I especially appreciate the practical, easy-to-understand approach Ron has maintained through these pages. His diagrams, worksheets, and illustrations, and even a glossary of terms take away all the mumbo jumbo, so that readers who lack sophisticated expertise in the field of economics have no trouble grasping and implementing his insights.

Having watched large audiences respond so enthusiastically to Ron's seminars and having experienced the benefits of his capable instruction personally, I am pleased to place my endorsement on this book. I recommend it to you without the slightest reservation.

If your desire is to "master your money" so that greater control and contentment begin to characterize your life, you have selected the right book. It won't take you long to realize that my friend has the right perspective on money, because he is in touch with the right Master.

—Chuck Swindoll
Pastor, Radio Bible Teacher, Author

PREFACE

Master Your Money was originally published in October of 1986. I am very grateful that many people read and benefited from it. Enough copies sold that a second edition was published in 1991. Between the first and second editions, much changed in our world. A significant stock market crash occurred in 1987. Eastern Europe and Russia have opened up economically and politically. The United States enjoyed a growing economy in the late 1980s and then a recession in the early 1990s as a war with Iraq started.

Between the second edition and the third edition in 1997, who could have foretold the changes as something called the Internet and the World Wide Web entered our lives? The stock market boomed to new highs; cell phones, pagers, and e-mail allowed virtually instant contact with anyone; inflation continued to remain low; and the U.S. economy showed unprecedented strength.

From the third edition in 1997 until this fourth edition in 2004, who could have imagined that the U.S. government would balance its budget and show a surplus, that interest rates would plummet to near-zero levels, and that Y2K would come and go without a technical glitch? The stock market kept booming until early 2000 and then nose-dived for three years. The United States was attacked on its own soil by terrorists in 2001, thus starting a war on terrorism. The war effort and the declining U.S. economy brought back large government deficits. Taxes were lowered to the lowest levels in generations.

As I have reviewed and revised *Master Your Money*, I have made many significant changes in the book to take into account our changed economic environment. The Bob and Laura illustrations have been updated, the tax chapter, the estate planning chapter, the investment chapter, and the insurance sections have been changed fairly dramatically to reflect changes in the economic environment and laws, as well as to reflect the changes of my own thinking.

What has struck me, however, in revising this book is how little has changed over the years, relative to money management and financial planning. I haven't changed any of the basic principles in this book. God's laws are timeless, regardless of changing economic situations. Despite all the major economic and global changes, His principles still work. They remain applicable, practical, and useful—whether in the twenty-first century or the next few centuries.

The success of this book—spanning two decades—is not due to my brilliance, or any new ideas, or my writing skills, or the writing skills of those who help me research and write. It is due to biblical principles. When they are applied to your life, you will overcome your money struggles and move toward financial freedom.

Acknowledgments

There are many to whom I owe a deep debt of gratitude, beginning with my wife, Judy, and five children, Cynthia, Denise, Karen, Tim, and Michael, who, in spite of suffering through the writing of this book, have given me constant encouragement and joy! It is because of my wife that I came to know Jesus Christ as my personal Savior, and her unswerving godly walk the last thirty-four years has been a source of spiritual encouragement and challenge.

Bruce Cook of Atlanta and Steve Douglass of Orlando, Florida, with whom I worked on the "I Found It" campaign, provided much of the material on goal setting and faith planning found throughout the book.

The late Larry Burkett; George and Marjean Fooshee of Wichita, Kansas; and Howard Dayton of Gainsville, Georgia, all wrote books on financial planning long before I did and had a major impact on my thinking as a financial advisor.

Chuck and Cynthia Swindoll have graciously given of their time and experience in helping me work through many of the difficult issues that come in tackling a project such as this.

I also want to acknowledge the contribution made by Jeremy White as he has made significant improvements in revising this book.

Lastly, but most importantly, my Lord and Savior, Jesus Christ, has again proved Himself to be faithful and apart from Him I would have nothing to say.

—Ron Blue

When I was beginning my career and marriage, I read a very important book in my personal and professional development—Ron Blue's *Master Your Money*. It helped me immensely to see my professional expertise through a biblical lens. It helped me personally and practically to budget and make better financial decisions. I gratefully acknowledge Ron as a mentor to me and to many others in the financial professions.

What an honor to now assist Ron with this newly revised edition of a classic! Because this book had such an impact on me, I have worked diligently to keep the essence of the timeless principles intact while striving to make this book even better, more relevant, and more up-to-date.

I would like to gratefully acknowledge my wife, Sharon, and daughters, Jenaye and Jaclyn, and their support during another of Daddy's writing projects. You are a great team to cheer me on when the going gets tough. God has given you three to me, and I consecrate to Him the love in my heart for you.

I would like to thank my office support team of Pam Estes and Kris White. You help make it possible for me to pull off these God-sized projects and still care for my clients.

—Jeremy White

WILL I EVER HAVE ENOUGH?

At the age of twenty-four, I had every ingredient needed for success—an MBA degree, my Certified Public Accountant (CPA) certificate, a well-paying job with the world's largest CPA firm in their New York City office, a driving ambition to be a success, and a supportive and very intelligent wife.

For the next eight years, I proved to myself that anyone could succeed by really putting everything into it. By the time I was thirty-two years old, I had achieved every financial and success goal I had set:

❖ I had moved rapidly up the corporate ladder.

❖ I had founded the fastest growing CPA firm in Indiana, and it became one of the fifty largest firms in the United States.

❖ I, along with others, owned two small banks in Indiana.

❖ I had a lovely wife and three young daughters.

❖ I had all of the trappings of success: a new home, new cars, country club memberships, and the like.

I had also just committed my life to Jesus Christ—a commitment that began to change my perspective and my priorities.

It was during the early 1970s, and for the first time in the nation's history, that Americans began experiencing "tremendous" inflation rates of 4 percent and 5 percent. The prime rate hit an unbelievable high of 10 percent and then even went to 12 percent. The dollar was taken off the gold standard, and for the first time in recent history, the United States began running a trade deficit.

In the midst of personal affluence, I began to experience the fear that comes from wondering, *Will I ever have enough?* Or, *If I do have enough now, will it be enough when I retire?* And, *By the way, how much is enough?* I believe that everyone, rich and poor, asks himself these underlying questions more frequently than he would like to admit. These questions are constantly in our subconscious, and therefore we all deal with them somehow in our decision making. Either we tend to hoard our resources, or we tend to live out the philosophy of "get all the *gusto* you can—you only go around once."

The Christian, *additionally,* is confronted with the question, What is the appropriate Christian lifestyle? This book, by the grace of God, will attempt to answer each of these questions by providing a framework of financial planning that is both biblical and relevant in our unique society.

Through the mid-1970s I dealt with these questions, both personally and as an advisor to a largely wealthy, secular clientele. In 1977 my wife, Judy, and I experienced God's call to leave the businesses I was involved in and join a new ministry in Atlanta, Georgia. For two years, as our family grew to five children, I helped to develop seminar materials in the areas of decision making, time management, faith planning, and problem solving. During this time, I traveled to Africa eleven times, assisting a large Christian organization to apply the principles that we were teaching.

I observed during all of this that the same financial questions my former clients and I had been asking were being asked by others as well: missionaries, affluent Africans, poor Africans, full-time Christian workers, successful American executives, pastors, and friends. The questions were:

- ❖ Will I ever have enough?

- ❖ Will it continue to be enough?

- ❖ How much is enough, particularly in view of my Christian convictions and understanding of Scripture?

The questions transcended cultures as well as classes.

In 1979, at the encouragement of Dr. Howard Hendricks, I began a financial planning career with the objective to remove the fear and frustration that Christians experience when they deal with money. The need for this type of counsel and advice is, I believe, *pervasive*. Christian teaching and application go from the extreme of sharing personal income in communal living to the "name it, claim it" approach. Both extremes are an attempt to *reach* God in the way we handle our money, when all the time He is attempting to reach out to us with His wisdom, counsel, and principles. I believe so strongly that American Christians need godly counsel for their finances that I now serve as president of Christian Financial Professionals Network (see appendix B and the website www.cfpn.org).

This book outlines the journey that Judy and I are on to "be filled with the knowledge of His will in all wisdom and spiritual understanding" (Colossians 1:9), as it specifically relates to personal money management for the Christian in the context of a very uncertain economic future.

The Rich and the Poor

In the world's most affluent society in all of history, very, very few individuals ever achieve a position of being able to live off the resources they have accumulated. The vast majority are dependent on government, relatives, or charity, or they must continue to work in order to have enough income to meet their needs. Yet there are exceptions, and I have had the privilege of meeting and working with many people who are better prepared for their future.

One of the dramatic exceptions is that of a retired pastor who never earned more than $8,000 in one year. I met this humble man because he wanted to know if he had enough financial resources to live out the rest of his life. At the time of his question, he was eighty years old; he had been retired for twenty years; and recently his wife had required full-time nursing care. His question, therefore, was a justifiable one!

As I generally do, I began to ask some questions before giving advice. First, I asked him if he had any debts. His response was no, and he went on to say he had never borrowed any money. I asked, "Why not?" He said because if he borrowed money, he would have to pay it back someday, and he couldn't afford to pay off debt, feed his family, and tithe.

My second question was to ask what resources he presently had. He indicated that in his wife's name, they had approximately $250,000 in cash, money market funds, and certificates of deposit. Additionally, in his name, they had another $350,000 in cash and cash-type investments. Needless to say, I was impressed! Over $600,000 in cash accumulated by a couple who had never earned more than $8,000 per year! And this was in 1982.

One thing bothered me though. He had not mentioned any stock investments, and yet in looking at his tax returns, I noticed a substantial amount of dividend income. He revealed that at retirement he had invested approximately $10,000 in the stock of a new company, and at the present time, the market value of his stock in that company was $1,063,000. WOW! $1,663,000 of cash and stock and they had never earned more than $8,000 per year!

This couple was unusual, but I know of many other couples who are headed in the same direction. They practice some very basic biblical principles that work regardless of the economy or economic environment. Incidentally, my advice to this man was not to seek advice from anyone, myself included, because we might "mess him up." I would be better off listening to him. This couple had followed four basic economic principles that will work for anyone regardless of the economic uncertainty. We will examine those principles in chapter 2.

Would this man have enough to live on? That was his question. Undoubtedly, he had enough to live on and to enjoy giving some away during his lifetime. We'll talk more about giving in chapter 15.

Debtors All

The years following World War II have seen an incredible growth in our affluence as a nation. No people, ever, have possessed the material resources that we do. We are truly a blessed people, and yet there are some significant cracks in our economic structure.

Our national debt (the amount of money owed by our government) is about $7,000,000,000,000![1] That's approximately $23,900 for every man, woman, and child in our country. If we wanted to pay off this debt, we would first of all have to stop going into debt; and then if we started a repayment plan of one $1,000,000 per day, it will still take over 3,500 years to pay back the debt (assuming there is no interest charged on the debt, which there is!). We have mortgaged not only our children's future, but also obligated countless future generations because of our lack of control and impatient spending. Someone must pay this debt through a literal repayment (future taxes), a deceitful repayment (future inflation), or cancellation (political upheaval). There are no other alternatives. The debt will not merely disappear.

I could go on and on about how serious our economic problems are. For example, what happens to our banking system if Third World countries refuse to pay their debts to American banks? What if the federal budget is not balanced? What happens to our economy if Japan's economy fails? The fact of the matter is, the problems are serious, and there is absolutely nothing that you or I, as individuals, can do to solve them.

While the original thirteen colonies were still part of Great Britain, Professor Alexander Tyler wrote of the Athenian Republic, which had fallen two thousand years earlier:

> A democracy cannot exist as a permanent form of government. It can only exist until the voters discover that they can vote themselves a largesse from the [public] treasury. From that moment on, the majority will always vote for the candidates promising the most benefits from the public treasury, with the result that a democracy always collapses over loose fiscal policy and is always followed by a dictatorship.

> The average age of the world's greatest civilizations has been 200 years. These nations have progressed through this sequence: From BONDAGE to SPIRITUAL FAITH; from SPIRITUAL FAITH to GREAT COURAGE; from GREAT COURAGE to ABUNDANCE; from ABUNDANCE to SELFISHNESS; from SELFISHNESS to COMPLA-

CENCY; from COMPLACENCY to APATHY; from APATHY to DE-
PENDENCY; from DEPENDENCY back again into BONDAGE.

There is no question that the United States is at least at the abundance level in the sequence outlined by Professor Tyler. In my opinion
we are leaving the selfishness level and approaching complacency.

Before you wring your hands in despair, let me give you a question to ponder. Do you think God is worried? Is He wringing His
hands in despair, wondering how it is all going to turn out? Of course
not! Inflation, deflation, monetary collapse, and political upheavals
are nothing new to Him; and His message is just as relevant today as
it has always been.

The context, therefore, of personal money management is that
God is still in control, and under His control there are four broad
economic situations: (1) inflation, (2) deflation, (3) monetary collapse, or (4) political upheaval. Although I am neither an economist
nor a prophet and I do not know what is going to happen, I can
plan for possible eventualities and base my planning on basic biblical financial principles. In the early 1980s, almost everyone was projecting increasing double-digit inflation. One of the consequences of
that belief was a rapid escalation in raw land prices, especially farmland. However, farmland can be purchased today for one-third to
one-half of what it was selling for in the early 1980s. Almost no one
predicted the collapse in farmland prices or oil prices, and the conse-
quent devastation to many families, corporations, and even cities. In
the early 2000s, economists have mentioned deflation in the midst of
the upheaval of the war on terrorism. The point is that neither inflation nor deflation is a sure thing. God is sovereign and can direct the
course of our economy in any way He wants.

In any case, financial planning *must* take place under the sover-
eignty of God, recognizing His omnipotence, wisdom, purposes, and
plans. Because there are only four economic possibilities, I must plan
for all *four* in answering three primary questions:

❖ Will I ever have enough?

❖ Will it continue to be enough?

❖ How much is enough?

I believe that God is more interested in each of us individually
than He is in any failure or success of our economic system. I do

not believe that the Bible sets forth any one economic system. God is interested in how I glorify Him wherever I live—whether under capitalism, communism, socialism, or any other system.

God has called each of us to a unique role in an uncertain economy. To be prepared for that role, we must understand the biblical principles of money management given in the next chapter.

Endnote:

1. Source: Bureau of the Public Debt, U.S. Treasury, 2004, http://www.publicdebt.treas.gov/opd/opdpenny.htm.

FOUR BIBLICAL PRINCIPLES OF MONEY MANAGEMENT

❦

"Money is a terrible master but an excellent servant."
P.T. BARNUM

"If a person gets his attitude toward money straight, it will help straighten out almost every other area of his life."
BILLY GRAHAM

"God can have our money and not have our hearts, but he cannot have our hearts without having our money."
R. KENT HUGHES

❦

An acquaintance of mine, William Cook, wrote a book called *Success, Motivation, and the Scriptures,* in which he defined *success* as "the continued achievement of being the person God wants me to be, and the continued achievement of established goals God helps me set."[1] I once asked my oldest child how her friends would define success, and she gave me the best worldly definition of success I have ever heard: "To have whatever you want whenever you want it."

One perspective is eternal and long-term, while the other is worldly and short-term: "I want what I want when I want it." Some even go further and believe, "Not only do I want what I want when I want it, but I have a right to it."

Both the Christian and non-Christian are concerned with success, and in each case success is always related to goals. The difference is in the perspective. One view sees only the here and now and self-promotion. The other sees the unseen eternity and the treasure to gain in heaven. What your perspective is (or to put it another way, what you believe) will determine attitudes and actions. That is why the Christian, in managing his or her money, is different.

Individually, God has called us to be *salt and light* (Matthew 5:13–16 NIV):

> You are the salt of the earth. But if the salt loses its saltiness, how can it be made salty again? It is no longer good for anything, except to be thrown out and trampled by men. You are the light of the world. A city on a hill cannot be hidden. Neither do people light a lamp and put it under a bowl. Instead they put it on its stand, and it gives light to everyone in the house. In the same way, let your light shine before men, that they may see your good deeds, and praise your Father in heaven.

He's called us to be *servants* (Mark 10:43–45); God has also called us to be *stewards* (Matthew 25:14–30).

The idea of being salt and light says that God wants me to be different from, not better than, others in the world. The Christian, therefore, may or may not have more than his neighbor, but that does not distinguish him. What does distinguish the Christian from the world is the absence of any anxiety, which might have come as a result of the loss of something he has managed or even God's denial of something he wants. Why? Because the Christian's treasure is not on earth. The world and its temporal toys do not possess him. He is prayerful. He plans. But he is not the least bit anxious about the uncertainty facing our national and world economy. He understands that Christ's promises of abundance do not mean financial security but peace and knowledge of Christ.

Such an attitude is not "normal" but rather "different," and it comes from having an entirely different perspective. The Christian's perspective is eternal, the attitude is one of holding possessions lightly, and the lifestyle is free from worry and anxiety. Truly that is different!

Not only have we been called to be salt and light, but all Christians have been called to be servants: "For even the Son of Man did not come to be served, but to serve, and to give His life a ransom for many" (Mark 10:45). Money is one of the most significant resources with which American Christians can serve others. It is not the only resource (time and talents are two others), but it is certainly in greater abundance among American Christians than among non-Americans.

By contrast, the world emphasizes serving yourself: "I want what I want when I want it." Advertising persuades us with "You deserve it." God says, "Command them to do good, to be rich in good deeds, and to be generous and willing to share" (1 Timothy 6:18 NIV).

Americans are known as generous people. But exactly how generous are we?

❖ According to the IRS, 1.7 percent of adjusted gross income is the average charitable deduction taken on Form 1040, whereas the property tax and interest deduction (as indicators of the possessions that the bank and I own) is equal to 18 percent of adjusted gross income.

❖ Sam Erickson of the Christian Legal Society once did a personal study of average charitable giving. His conclusion was that all Americans gave, on the average, 25 cents a day or $91 per year, and evangelical Christians gave an average of $1 a day or $365 per year.

❖ J. Robertson McQuilkin, past president of Columbia International University, pointed out in a speech that if members of the Southern Baptist denomination alone would give an average of $100 per year to foreign missions, over $1.4 billion per year would be given. They are nowhere near that level now. If they were, the fulfillment of the Great Commission could probably be financed rather easily in this generation by one denomination!

On the other hand, I personally know hundreds of Christians who are serving others by literally giving fortunes away. They have answered the question, why am I here? One reason you are here is to serve others, and if God has entrusted you with financial resources, you must use them to serve others. As the opening line of Rick Warren's best-selling book *The Purpose Driven Life* says, "It's not about you."

Ultimately, *financial planning is the predetermined use of financial resources in order to accomplish certain goals and objectives.* The difference in financial planning between the Christian and the non-

Christian is the source of the goals and objectives.

John MacArthur, pastor of Grace Community Church, Sun Valley, California, in his tape series "Mastery of Materialism" said, "[sixteen] out of Christ's 38 parables deal with money; more is said in the New Testament about money than heaven and hell combined; five times more is said about money than prayer; and while there are 500 plus verses on both prayer and faith, there are over 2,000 verses dealing with money and possessions." Obviously, the Bible has much to say about money management.

The Four Biblical Principles of Money Management

Even though the parable of the talents found in Matthew 25:14–30 deals primarily with Christ's return, it has shown me four basic biblical principles of money management that summarize much of what the Bible has to say regarding money and money management. If we can let these principles saturate our selfish hearts and become part of us, I believe we will be better prepared for accomplishing His purposes in this lifetime and better prepared for heaven.

1. God Owns It All

> Again, it will be like a man going on a journey, who called his servants and entrusted his property to them. —Matthew 25:14

Very few Christians would argue with the principle that God owns it all, and yet if we follow that principle to its natural conclusion, there are three revolutionary implications. First of all, God has the right to whatever He wants whenever He wants it. It is all His, because an owner has *rights;* I, as a steward, have only *responsibilities.* I may receive some benefits while maintaining my responsibilities, but the owner retains ownership.

When my oldest child reached driving age, she was very eager to use my car and, as her father, I entrusted my car to her. There was never any question that I could take back my car at any time for any reason. She had responsibilities. I maintained all the rights. But I, as the owner, gave her a great benefit by entrusting her with the car's use, and she returned that benefit with responsible use and care of the car. In the same way, every single possession that I have comes from someone else—God. I literally possess much but own nothing. God benefits me by sharing His property with me. I have a responsibility to Him to use it in a way that blesses and glorifies Him.

If you own your home, take a walk around your property to get a feel for the reality of this principle. Reflect on how long that dirt has been there and how long it will continue to be there; then ask yourself if you really own it or whether you merely possess it. You may have the title to it, but that title reflects your right to possess it temporarily, not forever. Only God literally owns it forever.

If I really believe that God owns it all, then when I lose any possession for whatever reason, my emotions may cry out, but my mind and spirit have not the slightest question as to God's right to take whatever He wants whenever He wants it. Really believing this also frees me to give generously of God's resources to God's purposes and His people. All that I have belongs to Him.

The second implication of God owning it all is that not only is my giving decision a spiritual decision, but *every spending decision is a spiritual decision.* There is nothing more spiritual than buying a car, taking a vacation, buying food, paying off debt, paying taxes, and so on. These are all responsible uses of His resources. He owns all that I have. He doesn't say I must use it all in one way, say as an offering. He doesn't say I must use it all the same way each time. He gives us resources to provide for us, benefit us, and reach the world for Christ. Many God-glorifying responsible uses fit into these broad categories.

Think about the freedom of knowing that if God owns it all—and He does—He must have some thoughts about how He wants me to use His property. The Bible reveals many specific guidelines as to how the Owner wants His property used. As a steward, I have a great deal of latitude, but I am still responsible to the Owner. Some day I will give an accounting of how I used His property.

The third implication of the truth that God owns it all is that *you can't fake stewardship.* Your checkbook reveals all that you really believe about stewardship. Your life story could be written from your checkbook. It reflects your goals, priorities, convictions, relationships, and even the use of your time. A person who has been a Christian for even a short while can fake prayer, Bible study, evangelism, and going to church, but he can't fake what his checkbook reveals. Maybe that is why so many of us are so secretive about our personal finances. Even within accountability groups where people share many intimate struggles, it is rare that anyone shares about how much (or how little) they give.

2. We Are in a Growth Process

His master replied, "Well done, good and faithful servant! You have been faithful with a few things; I will put you in charge of many things. Come and share your master's happiness!" —Matthew 25:21 NIV

In reading the Scriptures, we can't escape the truths that our time on earth is temporary and is to be used by our Lord. The whole parable emphasizes these truths. I believe that God uses money and material possessions in your earthly life during this growth process as *a tool, a test,* and *a testimony.* As Paul said in Philippians 4:11–12 NIV:

I am not saying this because I am in need, for I have learned to be content whatever the circumstances. I know what it is to be in need, and I know what it is to have plenty. I have learned the secret of being content in any and every situation, whether well fed or hungry, whether living in plenty or in want.

Money and material possessions are a very effective tool that God uses to help you grow. Therefore, you need always to ask, "God, what do You want me to learn?" You should not focus on asking (really a whine), "God, why are You doing this to me?" My role as a counselor has been to help people discover what God would have them learn, either from the situation of their abundance, or from the situation of their apparent lack of financial resources. God is not trying to frustrate us. He is trying to get our attention, and money is a great attention-getter.

Money is not only a tool, but also a test.

So if you have not been trustworthy in handling worldly wealth, who will trust you with true riches? And if you have not been trustworthy with someone else's property, who will give you property of your own? —Luke 16:11–12 NIV

I don't understand it, but I do know that somehow my eternal position and reward is determined irrevocably by my faithfulness in handling property that has been entrusted to me by God. And not only that, but this verse and others indicate that God trusts the true riches of knowing and understanding Him more to those who show their resolute commitment to Him in tangible ways, such as letting go of money or relationships.

We have already looked at the fact that in Matthew 5:13–16 we are called to be salt and light. I believe we can say that God can utilize my use of His resources as a testimony to the world. My attitude as a Christian toward wealth becomes the testimony. My attitude when He withholds a desire is also a testimony. My verbal praise when He arranges and allows financial blessings—or prevents my undoing—is also a testimony. Has He worked a financial miracle for you? Don't discount it as coincidence. Don't forget it years down the road when you have more affluence. Remember, rest, and revel in His answered prayer over financial matters; just don't let resentment creep in when things don't go your way in human terms. This is teaching time. This is testimony time. Have you failed in your use of God's money? What was your response to His "No"? What is your verbal witness of His involvement in your life? Don't let your first failure keep you so defeated that you talk yourself into failing again. Confess it, receive His mercy, and move on. You'll have another chance tomorrow. Remember, growth is a process, not a once-and-for-all. Jesus wants children who rely on Him, students who listen to Him, not grown-up graduates who don't need Him anymore.

3. The Amount Is Not Important

> His master replied, "Well done, good and faithful servant! You have been faithful with a few things; I will put you in charge of many things. Come and share your master's happiness!" —Matthew 25:23 NIV

When you look back to verse 21 and compare it word for word with verse 23, you will see that the same words were spoken to the slave with five talents and to the one with two talents. Both were reminded that they had been faithful with a few things and both were promised something as a reward. You can draw the conclusion that the amount you have is unimportant, but how you handle what you have been entrusted with is very important.

There is much controversy today about whether an American Christian is more spiritual on one hand by accumulating much (God's "blessing"), or on the other hand by giving it all away (God's "martyr"). I believe that both are extremes and not reflective of what God says. He neither condemns wealth nor commends poverty, or vice versa. The principle found in Scripture is that He owns it all. Therefore, whatever He chooses to entrust you with, hold with an open hand, allowing Him to entrust you with more if He so chooses, or allowing Him to take whatever He wants. It is all His. That is the attitude He wants you to develop, and whatever you have, little or much, your attitude should remain the same.

4. Faith Requires Action

> Then the man who had received the one talent came. "Master," he said, "I knew that you are a hard man, harvesting where you have not sown and gathering where you have not scattered seed. So I was afraid and went out and hid your talent in the ground. See, here is what belongs to you." His master replied, "You wicked, lazy servant! So you knew that I harvest where I have not sown and gather where I have not scattered seed? Well then, you should have put my money on deposit with the bankers, so that when I returned I would have received it back with interest. Take the talent from him and give it to the one who has the ten talents. For everyone who has will be given more, and he will have an abundance. Whoever does not have, even what he has will be taken from him. And throw that worthless servant outside, into the darkness, where there will be weeping and gnashing of teeth."
>
> —Matthew 25:24–30 NIV

The wicked slave knew better, *but* he did nothing. Many of us know what we ought to do, but we disobey or delay. We have emotional faith and/or intellectual faith, but not active faith. We know, *but . . .*

We may know deep down what God would have us do, but we are so bombarded with worldly input, which seems to be acceptable, that we are paralyzed. We take no action because of the fear of making a mistake biblically or financially. Or we are frustrated and confused. We do only what we feel good about. Living by our feelings rather than "the truth" can be very dangerous. "Jesus answered, 'I am the way and the truth and the life. No one comes to the Father except through me'" (John 14:6 NIV).

The Practicality of Stewardship

I will be giving you principles, technical guidance, tools, and techniques for working out *by faith* the unique financial plan that God has for you and your family, so that when you stand before Him you will have confidence and expect Him to say, "Well done, good and faithful servant." Is that hope unrealistic? Not at all. It is God's desire and His intention. He wants to say it more than you want to hear it.

Before we go any further, let me summarize these biblical principles of money management. First, let's establish a working definition of stewardship:

⬦⬦⬦

Stewardship is the use of God-given resources for the accomplishment of God-given goals.

⬦⬦⬦

This definition is active, not theoretical. It says "use of." Remember that faith requires action. This view of stewardship acknowledges God's ownership over my possessions and His direction of my use of them.

Second, on page 28, I would like for you to list anything that you now possess, about which until now you would have said, "This is mine." Then return the ownership of it to its rightful Owner by a simple prayer of commitment. Sign the deed and date it.

You now own nothing and are prepared to be a steward.

Endnote:

1. William H. Cook, *Success, Motivation, and the Scriptures* (Nashville: Broadman Press, 1974), p. 44.

Deed

*On this date I/we acknowledge God's ownership and my/our
stewardship responsibility of the following:*

ITEM	AMOUNT

DATE   SIGNATURE

A FINANCIAL PLANNING OVERVIEW

"O money, money, money, I'm not necessarily one of those who thinks thee holy, but I often stop to wonder how thou canst go out so fast when thou comest in so slowly."
OGDEN NASH

"A wise man should have money in his head, but not in his heart."
JONATHAN SWIFT

"Make all you can, save all you can, give all you can."
JOHN WESLEY

"A man's treatment of money is the most decisive test of his character—how he makes it and how he spends it."
MOFFAT

hen my children were young, each year for Christmas I gave them two sheets of paper as a gift. On the sheets I listed several things I could do with them during the next year. Some of the options included: going out for breakfast or lunch; going to a professional baseball, basketball, or football game; or going with me on one of my speaking trips. My objective was to let them pick how they would really like to spend time with me.

It was interesting to observe the difficulty they had in choosing which activity they really wanted. They seemed to choose frequently the option "spending four hours with me and having $25 to spend in any way you choose." The first year we began this tradition my third daughter, nine years old at the time, picked this option and carefully planned our time together. We were to start at a large shopping mall on a Saturday morning and end with lunch. She was filled with anticipation and excitement when the day arrived.

Picture in your mind a nine-year-old child with $25 in her hand, entering a mall with tens of millions of dollars' worth of goods available to buy. The dilemma she faced is exactly the same dilemma that you and I face—there is *never* enough money to do or buy everything that you want. There are always more ways to spend money than there is money available. You may respond as she did.

After shopping for just a little while, we went in a store with overpriced notions, such as crazy pens, note paper, and so on, and she selected several items—despite my caution that tomorrow they would not be nearly as attractive. I said to her, "Honey, remember that good decision making requires a long-term perspective." She assured me that she would use and love these items "forever and ever." When the bill was totaled, she had spent her $25, and we still had three hours left and lunch to buy. We ended up going home early so that she could play with her purchases.

The very next day everything she had purchased was either used up, broken, or uninteresting. I will never forget her confessing to me that she had, in effect, responded to the emotion of the moment and, in retrospect, made a poor choice. The problem was that her money and time were both irretrievably lost.

What was not lost, however, was the experience and what it taught her. Later when I was getting ready to buy something, she frequently said to me, "Daddy, don't forget that the longer term your perspective, the better your decision is likely to be." Sometimes I wish that I hadn't taught her that!

This story illustrates four truths:

1. All of us have limited resources.

2. Consequently, more uses of money are available than money available.

3. Today's decisions determine destiny. (A dollar spent is gone forever and can never be used in the future for anything else.)

4. The longer term the perspective, the better potential for wise decisions.

I can summarize these four points by saying that most of us are responders rather than planners. We respond to friends, advertising, and our emotions rather than plan our spending.

◇◇

**Financial planning is allocating limited
financial resources among
unlimited alternatives.**

◇◇

When we know for certain what financial resources we have and plan to use them to accomplish God-given goals and objectives, we live in peace and contentment from making order out of chaos. Our frustration in having to choose among overwhelming choices disappears. We are freed from the pressures of the short-term, self-gratifying society around us. We are free to be different.

The financial planning framework that I am going to help you develop will do several things. It will give you a process of managing money; summarize the almost infinite uses of money into just a manageable few; integrate short-term and long-term planning and clearly demonstrate their trade-offs. It will also give you a sense of order and thereby remove some of the guilt or confusion in managing money.

Objectives of Financial Planning

One principle I have been implying all along but have never actually stated is that accumulating financial resources should never be an end in itself. They are accumulated solely for the reason of using them to accomplish some purpose, goal, or objective. For example, you do not take a vacation or buy a car just to spend money, but rather to provide something else such as recreation or transportation. Many people ask me how to spend money, and I always make it a practice to ask, "What are you really trying to accomplish?" This question helps to focus the decision on real objectives.

In the short term, there are basically only five spending objectives; in the long term, only six. Every spending decision or use of money accomplishes one of these eleven objectives.

Short-term Objectives

Figure 3.1 illustrates that there are only five short-term uses for all income coming into a household:

1. Given away
2. Spent to support a lifestyle
3. Used for the repayment of debt
4. Used to meet tax obligations
5. Saved (cash-flow margin)

Short-term Uses of Income

Figure 3.1

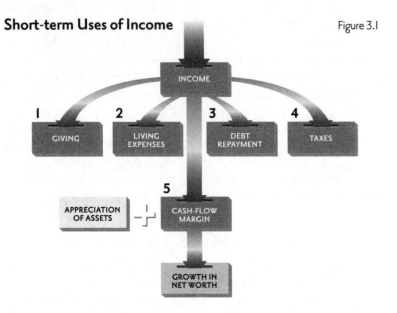

Every spending decision, in the short term, will fit into one of these five categories.

How my money is allocated among the five categories is a function of just two factors: the commitments I already have and my priorities. For example, with my wife and five children, I had certain lifestyle commitments that others did not have. Debt repayment, taxes, and giving are all commitments I had to maintain. As time passed, those commitments changed as my family situation and career changed. Certain lifestyle expenses such as utilities, food, insurance, and so on are also commitments. A commitment must always be top priority.

Ultimately, my priorities dictate the use of my remaining resources. Many people would state their priorities are giving and saving, but in reality, these uses wind up at the bottom of the priority ladder. I have observed that most American Christians have lifestyle as their top priority, and second, because of their lifestyle, debt repayment. Taxes would be a third priority because they have no choice; fourth would be saving; and finally, giving. The flawed line of reasoning goes this way: *I am already committed to a certain lifestyle and debt schedule, which God surely wouldn't want me to change. I would gladly give up paying my taxes, but I can't. I am giving and would give more if it weren't for the taxes I have to pay and the money I need to set aside for the future because that is good stewardship.*

Of the five short-term uses, three are consumptive in nature and two are productive. Lifestyle expenditures, debt repayment, and taxes are all consumptive in nature; when the money is spent, it is gone forever. Both saving and giving are productive uses of money. Money that is put into saving is much like planting a crop—later on, much more than what was planted comes up and can be used again for either consumption or production.

The Bible gives us many principles and guidelines about each one of these five areas, but very little in the way of direct commandment. To determine what God would have us do in balancing our priorities requires the discipline of spending time with Him. No one other person, including your financial planner, can tell you how to prioritize your spending. Why? God has not entrusted the resources you possess (but do not own) to someone else; only *you* are accountable for managing the use of God's resources entrusted to you.

Long-term Objectives

In reviewing figure 3.1, you will note that as we save from our cash-flow margin, we grow our net worth—not for the sake of big numbers, but for the purpose of meeting one of our long-term objectives. The more common long-term objectives include the following:

1. Financial independence
2. College education for children
3. Paying off debt
4. Major lifestyle desires
5. Major charitable giving

6. Owning your own business

To be financially independent means that the resources accumulated will generate enough income to fund all of the short-term objectives, with the exception of savings, for your life span. (Savings are no longer needed if "enough" has been accumulated.) When a couple knows what their short-term objectives are, they can easily calculate how large an investment fund is necessary to accumulate what they need in order to be financially independent.

In addition to accumulating for financial independence, couples with children often have the long-term objective of assisting their children in paying some of their college education. Although nearly grown children may contribute to the cost of college through their own work and savings, many parents want to limit the amount of student-loan debt their children incur. Saving and wise investing are necessary in order to meet the major expense of college education—an expense that can easily reach $15,000–$20,000 per year for each child.

Many couples also have a major long-term goal of being completely out of debt, including the debt on their home. We will discuss the whole issue of debt in chapter 6, but I believe it is a worthwhile long-term objective to be totally debt free.

The long-term objective of major lifestyle desires is the area that makes each family unique. The objective could be a different home, a second home, a new car, a particular vacation, redecorating or remodeling the home. This type of goal finishes the statement: "I want to improve my lifestyle by . . ."

One of the first clients with whom I worked was a man who indicated that the most important long-term goal he could think of was to be able to give away at least one million dollars toward the fulfillment of the Great Commission. This was the first time I had ever considered that people may desire to accumulate over the long-term in order to meet a substantial giving goal. This man not only wanted to give the one million dollars before retirement, but he wanted to continue to give at approximately 15 percent of his total income during the time period that he would be accumulating wealth. He had specific long-term and short-term objectives when it came to giving.

Lastly, you may want to save in order to start your own business, and that is also a legitimate long-range goal.

If you can define and quantify these long-term goals, then you will have answered the question: How much is enough? You know now what your "finish lines" are. It is much like a runner who runs the race until he breaks the tape. Very few runners continue after they have broken the tape. Yet in our financial lives, many of us never stop running because we do not know where the finish line is. We have never quantified where we are headed, and therefore we do not know when we have arrived.

My challenge to you is to determine where you are going, both in the short-term and in the long-term.

Integrated Planning

Figure 3.2 puts together the short-term and long-term objectives and outlines a four-step process of financial planning.

Step 1: Summarize your present situation.

Step 2: Establish your financial goals.

Step 3: Plan to increase your cash-flow margin.

Step 4: Control your cash flow.

I will take you through each step to develop your own unique financial plan in the chapters ahead. If you know where you are, where you are going, and the steps to get there, then you will have made a major step toward being a planner rather than a responder, being proactive rather than reactive.

As you review the figure, there are three very important implications. The first is that *there are no independent financial decisions.* If you make a decision to use financial resources in any one area, by definition, you have chosen not to use those same resources in the other areas. This means that if you choose to set aside money for college education or financial independence, you no longer have that money available to spend on giving, lifestyle desires, debt repayment, and the like. By the same token, if you decide to spend money on lifestyle desires, you no longer have those same resources available for any other short-term or long-term goals.

The second implication when looking at that figure is that *the longer term perspective you have, the better the possibility of making a good financial decision now.* A friend and close confidant once defined financial maturity as "being able to give up today's desires for

The Financial Planning Process

Figure 3.2

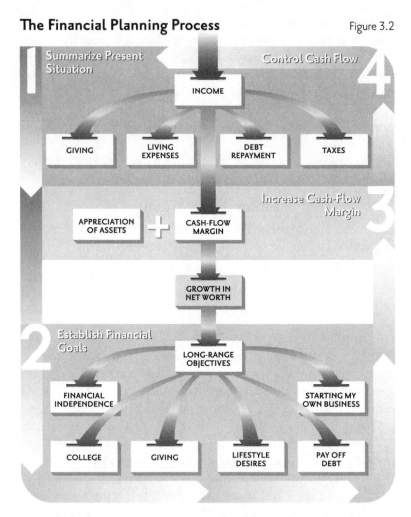

future benefits." If I choose to give up something today in order to save for tomorrow, I have probably made a wise financial decision. The most dramatic example I can think of is the person who chooses a husband or wife. Taking a long-term perspective in that decision makes for a better choice than simply satisfying a short-term need. The same principle holds true in financial decisions.

The third implication of this Financial Planning Process is *the lifetime nature of financial decisions.* I mentioned earlier that three uses of money in the short-term are consumptive and two are productive.

Whenever money is used consumptively, it is gone forever and can never be used for anything in the future. I like to remind those with whom I counsel that *decisions determine destiny*. Once I make a decision either to save or spend, I have determined, to some extent, my financial destiny.

You, of course, have to accept the truth of this implication—you can't have everything you want when you want it. A key to success is knowing where you are going in life and knowing how to arrive there. These goal areas, however, are not what we are really trying to accomplish in life, but rather reflect the real desires of our hearts:

- ❖ Security
- ❖ Properly trained children
- ❖ Peace
- ❖ Contentment
- ❖ Flexibility
- ❖ Comfort
- ❖ Personal growth
- ❖ Obedience to God
- ❖ Transportation
- ❖ Rest and relaxation
- ❖ Self-worth
- ❖ Acceptance
- ❖ Sense of belonging
- ❖ Other goals . . .

Money, then, is one of the resources you use to accomplish the desires you have. Success is knowing what God would have you be and do, and how to achieve that, so that when you stand before Him, you will hear Him say, "Well done, good and faithful servant." When money becomes your focus, you are doomed to disappointment, because money is merely a resource and was never intended by the Creator to be anything more than that.

GUARANTEED FINANCIAL SUCCESS

"Money talks . . . but all mine ever says is good-bye."
ANONYMOUS

"If you would be wealthy, think of saving rather than getting."
BENJAMIN FRANKLIN

"It is thrifty to prepare today for the wants of tomorrow."
AESOP, "THE ANT AND THE GRASSHOPPER"

I remember once walking from the Sunday morning worship service to my Sunday school class when a teacher stopped me to ask if I could help him with his lesson on stewardship for that morning. The class was to start in just a few minutes, but I agreed to tell him all I could in that brief time. I said a quick prayer asking for wisdom, and the thought came that my stewardship message is threefold.

1. **God owns it all.**

2. **Money is never an end in itself, but is merely a resource to accomplish other goals and obligations.**

3. **Spend less than you earn and do it for a long time, and you will be financially successful.**

There is tremendous freedom of mind in knowing and believing that God owns it all, and that money is nothing more than a resource provided by God to allow us to accomplish His purposes on this earth.

Is it wrong then to have a long-term goal of financial independence? I believe not—unless financial independence is defined as having enough to be independent from God. This whole question is really, how much is enough?

How do you achieve one or more of the long-term goals, such as financial independence, college education, improving your lifestyle, getting out of debt, making major contributions, or starting your own business? The answer is simple: Spend less than you earn and do it for a long time, or as the Bible says, "He who gathers money little by little makes it grow" (Proverbs 13:11 NIV).

For example, if you started supporting yourself at age twenty and for the next forty years you always spent $1,000 less than you earned, and you invested that $1,000 each year in an investment returning at least 12.5 percent, at age sixty you would have an investment fund of $1,000,000. (This computation is for an illustration of the power of compounding and ignores the tax implications, which we will deal with later, and current yields in most investments.)

Or if you are already at age forty, you can spend $10,000 per year less than you earn, invest it at a 12.5 percent return, and you can still accumulate the $1,000,000 by age sixty. The 12.5 percent and $1,000,000 are neither magical nor necessarily even desirable, but they do illustrate what has been called the eighth wonder of the world—the "magic of compounding."

The magic of compounding results from the relationship between an interest rate and a time period that can be determined by the "Rule of 72." The Rule of 72 says that any interest rate divided into 72 will always give you the length of time required for an amount to double in value. For example, if you invest $10,000 at an interest rate of 3 percent, it will take twenty-four years for the $10,000 to grow to $20,000.

$$72 \div 3\% = 24 \text{ years}$$

If, however, I can earn 6 percent, the $10,000 will double in only twelve years.

$$72 \div 6\% = 12 \text{ years}$$

To observe the magic of compounding, observe in this chart that as you double the interest rate earned, you get a geometric increase in the amount accumulated.

Rule of 72

Chart 4-A

RATE		YEAR 1	YEAR 12	YEAR 24	YEAR 36	YEAR 48	RESULT
	3%	$10,000		$20,000		$40,000	
Double							
	6%	10,000	$20,000	40,000	$80,000	160,000	4 times greater
Double							
	12%	10,000	40,000	160,000	640,000	2,560,000	16 times greater
Double							
	24%	10,000	160,000	2,560,000	40,960,000	655,360,000	256 times greater

The magic of compounding results because interest earns interest, which earns interest, which earns interest, which earns interest, *ad infinitum*. In other words, the amount is not nearly so important as the interest rate and the time period. The earlier you start and the more you earn in interest, *the less you need to start with.*

How important is the interest rate? Look at chart 4-B. At 25 percent, $10,000 grows to $75,231,638 in forty years, but at 24 percent, it only grows to $54,559,126 in the same length of time, nearly a $21,000,000 difference.

When you look at chart 4-C and compare the deposit of an annual amount with the deposit of a lump sum in chart 4-B, you immediately see that it takes much more money over a longer time period to achieve the same results. Ten thousand dollars invested initially and never added to, but growing at a compounded rate of 25 percent per year, grows to $75,231,638; whereas $1,000 invested per year for forty years or a total of $40,000 invested (four times as much) only "grows" to $30,088,655.

Compounding always involves four items—the amount available, the amount needed, the time period, and the earnings rate. If I know three of the variables, I can always determine the fourth from one of the charts.

Let's assume you have a child who will be starting college in ten years, and you would like to be able to provide $20,000 toward his college education and let him provide the balance in some way—scholarships, savings, or work. If you can save $1,000 per year toward that goal, the question is, what earnings rate do you have to achieve?

Chart 4-B

Compounding Time + Money + Yield
INVESTING A LUMP SUM OF $10,000:

%	5	10	15	20	25	30	35	40
2%	$11,041	$12,190	$13,459	$14,859	$16,406	$18,114	$19,999	$22,080
4%	12,167	14,802	18,009	21,911	26,658	32,434	39,460	48,010
6%	13,382	17,908	23,966	32,071	42,919	57,435	76,861	102,857
8%	14,693	21,589	31,722	46,610	68,485	100,627	147,853	217,245
10%	16,105	25,937	41,772	67,275	108,347	174,494	281,024	452,593
12%	17,623	31,058	54,736	96,463	170,001	299,599	527,996	930,510
14%	19,254	37,072	71,379	137,435	264,619	509,502	981,002	1,888,835
16%	21,003	44,114	92,655	194,608	408,742	858,499	1,803,141	3,787,212
18%	22,878	52,338	119,737	273,930	626,686	1,433,706	3,279,973	7,503,783
20%	24,883	61,917	154,070	383,376	953,962	2,373,763	5,906,682	14,697,716
22%	27,027	73,046	197,423	533,576	1,442,101	3,897,579	10,534,018	28,470,378
24%	29,316	85,944	251,956	738,641	2,165,420	6,348,199	18,610,540	54,559,126
25%	30,518	93,132	284,217	867,362	2,646,978	8,077,936	24,651,903	75,231,638

Chart 4-C

End-of-year Values
$1,000 DEPOSITED EACH YEAR:

%	5	10	15	20	25	30	35	40
2%	$5,204	$10,950	$17,293	$24,297	$32,030	$40,568	$49,994	$60,402
4%	5,416	12,006	20,024	29,778	41,646	56,085	73,652	95,026
6%	5,637	13,181	23,276	36,786	54,865	79,058	111,435	154,762
8%	5,867	14,487	27,152	45,762	73,106	113,283	172,317	259,057
10%	6,105	15,937	31,772	57,275	98,347	164,494	271,024	442,593
12%	6,353	17,549	37,280	72,052	133,334	241,333	431,663	767,091
14%	6,610	19,337	43,842	91,025	181,871	356,787	693,573	1,342,025
16%	6,877	21,321	51,660	115,380	249,214	530,312	1,120,713	2,360,757
18%	7,154	23,521	60,965	146,628	342,603	790,948	1,816,652	4,163,213
20%	7,442	25,959	72,035	186,688	471,981	1,181,882	2,948,341	7,343,858
22%	7,740	28,657	85,192	237,989	650,955	1,767,081	4,783,645	12,936,535
24%	8,048	31,643	100,815	303,601	898,092	2,640,916	7,750,225	22,728,803
25%	8,207	33,253	109,687	342,945	1,054,791	3,227,174	9,856,761	30,088,655

Known Variables:
Amount desired $20,000
Time period   10 years
Amount provided $1,000

1. Go to chart 4-C (deposit of an annual amount).

2. Look down the 10-year column and find the number closest to $20,000 ($21,321).

3. Determine which row you are in—16%.

Solution—Required earnings rate 16%.

If 16 percent cannot be reasonably achieved, then more than $1,000 per year must be invested or the amount accumulated will not reach the goal. Then, you must seek alternative funding sources for college.

Using the following form, you can go through this same exercise with each of your long-term goals:

Long-term Goals   Chart 4-D

	AMOUNT NEEDED	WHEN NEEDED	AMOUNT AVAILABLE	EARNINGS RATE
Financial Independence	$		$	
College Education				
Pay Off Debt				
Major Lifestyle Desires				
Car				
Home				
Vacation				
Other				
Giving				
Start Own Business				

At the end of this chapter are several examples (see page 48) you can experiment with, but here is the key point: **You do not have to save $1,000,000 to end up with $1,000,000.** The earlier you start, the less you have to save. The later you start, the more you either have to save or earn in interest (and therefore take more risk).

At this point, you are saying to yourself one or more of the following:

❖ Why didn't I hear this earlier? It's too late for me.

❖ Yes, but where can I earn 25 percent?

❖ In forty years $75,000,000 won't be worth much because of inflation.

❖ He has ignored that I must pay taxes on the interest every year; therefore, the compounding won't work as illustrated.

❖ I don't care about the future; I want to enjoy the money now.

Financial Planning Diagram

Figure 4.1

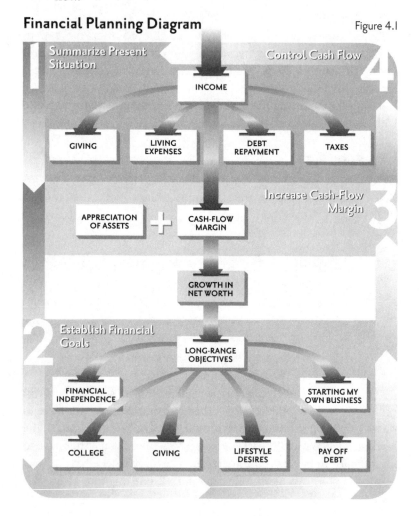

Let me assure you that not only do I understand these comments, but in some cases, I am still dealing with them on a personal level. All of them will be addressed in the balance of this chapter and the next, but first you must not only understand "the magic of compounding" but also the concept of "margin."

The Concept of Margin

Dr. Richard A. Swenson wrote a book called *Margin/The Overload Syndrome: Learning to Live Within Your Limits*. His key idea is to find time to rest and space to heal when feeling tired, worn out, or burned out. We can apply this same concept of margin to our financial lives.

The retired pastor described in chapter 1 pointed out to me the guaranteed key to financial success when he said that he "never spent more than he earned." He always tithed, paid his taxes, and lived on what was left.

Look again at our Financial Planning Diagram (see figure 4.1) and observe that, first of all, the long-term goals will probably require substantial financial resources; and second, that without receiving either an inheritance or striking oil, the only way to reach your long-term goals is to spend less than you earn over time. In other words, you must plan to have a cash-flow margin every year. When you do this and let the magic of compounding work for you, you can reach your long-term goals if you start early enough.

However, like most of us, you probably already have short-term commitments and priorities that may have you spending more than you earn or mandate that both spouses must work. Perhaps you are funding your annual negative cash-flow margin with increased credit card or other consumer debt. Incidentally, consumer debt is so easy to get because the lenders of money understand very well the magic of compounding. For example, if you pay a lender $1,000 per year for car payments every year during a working life (about forty years), and the lender in turn lends out your payment to another borrower at 12.5 percent interest, the lender will have accumulated $1,000,000 from your mere $40,000 of car payments.

$1,000,000 − $40,000 = $960,000—the interest earned.

$960,000 ÷ 40 = $24,000—the average interest earned per year.

The point is that you want the magic of compounding working for you instead of against you, and that will happen only if you spend less than you earn. It's better to be a lender than a borrower. You *must* have a cash-flow margin in order to achieve your long-term financial goals.

To create or increase your margin, you only have two choices: *increase income* or *decrease expenses*. You or your spouse could take on another job, work overtime, or start a business to create income. But the extra time away from family and stress may make family life more difficult.

The other option, and usually the better one, is to reduce expenses. This is the hard part, because in order to generate enough cash-flow margin each year to meet your long-term goals, you have to make the long term a priority over the short term (delayed gratification). So where do you cut? The tithe should not be cut; taxes cannot be cut without either reducing your income or spending cash on some deductible item; debt repayment cannot and should not be cut. The main area left is your lifestyle. However, many lifestyle expenses cannot be cut because of previous commitments, such as where you live, how many mouths you have to feed, and so on. The world, in the form of advertisers, friends, neighbors, other Christians, and even Christian leaders, would lead you to believe that you are owed or have a right to a lifestyle that may very well be beyond what you can afford.

I believe it is easy to know what lifestyle God has chosen for you by working through the following chart:

Amount Available for Lifestyle

Chart 4-E

TOTAL INCOME		$
Less Tithe	—	
Less All Taxes	—	
Less Debt Repayment	—	
Less Savings for Long-term	—	
BALANCE		$

The balance left is the amount available for the funding of a lifestyle. Granted, this may seem simplistic, but God's answers don't have to be difficult. It is also true that you may not achieve the lifestyle level you are seeking immediately, that the tithe is just the beginning of giving and in time you will give more, that planning can affect the amount paid in taxes, and that God may choose to increase your income. But to presume any of these things will happen is a violation of a biblical principle (see James 4:13–17).

The point is that you must plan to have a cash-flow margin if you are going to achieve your long-term goals, and the only truly discretionary place to cut spending, in order to generate this margin, is in the area of lifestyle. However, to do so will be very, very, very difficult because there will be no worldly support and very little Christian support. Frankly, only by the grace of God can it be done. In chapter 9, I will share with you ways to reduce living expenses, and in chapter 6, I will show you how to get out of debt and stay out. (Living expenses and debt are intertwined in American society.)

Conclusion

Adding the concept of cash-flow margin with the magic of compounding equals these conclusions:

1. *Get rich slowly.* Accumulation of financial resources is not difficult—it merely requires patience and self-discipline; both are fruits of the Spirit. It is not necessary to save $1,000,000 in order to have a $1,000,000. Again, *I am not suggesting that this should even be your goal,* but rather, that accumulation for long-term goals is not nearly as difficult as one might think. The Bible says, "He who gathers money little by little makes it grow"; and I would paraphrase that to say, "You can't eat an elephant in one bite, but you can eat an elephant one bite at a time."

2. *There is an opportunity cost to consumption.* A dollar spent today does *not* take a dollar out of the future; it takes *multiple* dollars. Only $2.74 per day spent on nonproductive purchases results in an overspending of $1,000 per year. If that $1,000 per year were instead invested so as to earn 12.5 percent compounded annually (such as in an IRA), then the $2.74 per day cost me the $1,000,000 that I could have had. The next time you make a spontaneous purchase, ask yourself, what does this really cost me in the future? Likewise, losses on investments or mistakes on major purchases, such as cars, cost far more than they appear, because not only must the loss be made up but also what that loss would have earned in the intervening time must be made up.

3. *Money has time value.* The amount that I have today is worth far more in the future than it is today, assuming that it can earn something each year.

Compounding Problems and Solutions

Table 4.1

EXAMPLE 1: Required earnings rate

Known Variables:

Amount available ....$1,000 per year

Amount needed..$100,000

When needed (time period) ....20 years

SOLUTION—Earnings rate—16%

1. Go to chart 4-C, page 42 (deposit of an annual amount).

2. Come down the 20-year column to the number closest to $100,000.

3. Go across to the earnings rate percentage to see what percentage is required.

EXAMPLE 2: Time it will take to accumulate a required amount

Known Variables:

Amount available ....$10,000 now

Amount needed..$50,000

Earnings rate attainable 8%

SOLUTION—Time required—20 years plus

1. Go to chart 4-B, page 42 (deposit of a lump sum).

2. Come down the earnings rate column to 8%.

3. Go across to find the amount closest to $50,000.

4. Determine which "years" column you are in.

EXAMPLE 3: Amount that will be accumulated

Known Variables:

Amount available ....$5,000 per year

Earnings rate attainable 12%

Time period I can save and earn ....15 years

SOLUTION—Amount that will be accumulated—$186,400

1. Go to chart 4-C (deposit of an annual amount).

2. Come down the 15-year column to the point where it inter-sects the 12% row and determine the number—$37,280.

3. Multiply the number $37,280 × 5 ($5,000 per year is 5 × $1,000 per year).

EXAMPLE 4: How much needs to be invested each year

Known Variables:

Amount needed..$50,000

Earnings rate attainable 10%

When needed (time period) ....10 years

SOLUTION—Amount required to be invested each year—$3,137

1. Go to chart 4-C (deposit of an annual amount).

2. Find the number at the intersection of the 10-year column and 10% row ($15,937). This is the amount that $1,000 in-vested each year at 10% earnings rate will grow to.

3. Divide $50,000 by $15,937 and multiply the result 3.137 × $1,000. In other words, it takes 3.137 × $1,000 per year to achieve $50,000 in 10 years at an earnings rate of 10%, since $1,000 per year at 10% for 10 years will only grow to $15,937.

THE MYTHS OF
INFLATION

*"What some people mistake for the high cost of living is really
the cost of high living."*
DOUG LARSON

"In spite of the cost of living, it's still popular."
LAURENCE J. PETER

*"Inflation is the one form of taxation that can be imposed
without legislation."*
MILTON FRIEDMAN

Over the last several years I have
had the privilege of traveling all over this country and speaking to
thousands of people. At some point during many of my presentations, I often ask everyone in the audience who believes that inflation is dead to raise his or her hand. To date, absolutely no one has ever raised a hand, and yet inflation is relatively low today, especially when compared to the late 1970s and early 1980s. As I stated earlier, I am not a prophet. Nevertheless, I believe the very basic greedy nature of human beings will force inflation on our society, and there is little that you and I can do about it except plan for it.

A good description of the effects of inflation is found in Haggai 1:6 (NIV): "You have planted much, but have harvested little. You eat, but never have enough. You drink, but never have your fill. You put on clothes, but are not warm. You earn wages, only to put them in a purse with holes in it."

Inflation Illustration: Future Equivalents

Chart 5-A

YEARS TO RETIREMENT	EXPECTED INFLATION RATE					
	2%	4%	6%	8%	10%	12%
5	1.10	1.22	1.34	1.47	1.61	1.76
10	1.22	1.48	1.79	2.16	2.59	3.11
15	1.35	1.80	2.40	3.17	4.18	5.47
20	1.49	2.19	3.21	4.66	6.73	9.65
25	1.64	2.67	4.29	6.85	10.83	17.00
30	1.81	3.24	5.74	10.06	17.45	29.96
35	2.00	3.95	7.69	14.79	28.10	52.90
40	2.21	4.80	10.29	21.73	45.26	93.05

The problem with inflation is twofold, and both problems cause fear. First of all, inflation destroys the purchasing power of the money already accumulated; and second, it requires that you continually earn more just to stay even with the increasing costs for the goods and services you need to live on. This is true because inflation has a compounding effect that makes the magic of compounding work against us.

For example, you can look at the different inflation assumptions in chart 5-A and determine what income you will need at retirement in order to have the same relative income as you have now. A couple earning $30,000 a year now will have to earn 5.74 times as much, or $172,200 a year, in thirty years just to have the same relative income, if we have an inflation rate of merely 6 percent. If the inflation rate for those thirty years is 10 percent rather than 6 percent (only 4 percent more), the relative increase will need to be 17.45 times $30,000, or $523,500.

It is no wonder that Dwight Eisenhower identified inflation as one of the major problems facing our nation when he left office in 1960—and the inflation rate then was a mere 1.5 percent! In fact, high levels of inflation in our country are a very recent phenomenon. Look at figure 5.1.

The problem is not so much inflation as it is the fear of inflation. One of the results of this fear of the future is that we have become a "now" society. Too many of us adopt the philosophy that it will never be any cheaper than it is now, and besides, we only go around once.

Out of this fear and emphasis on the now have evolved four basic myths regarding inflation. They are: (1) Buy it now, because it will cost

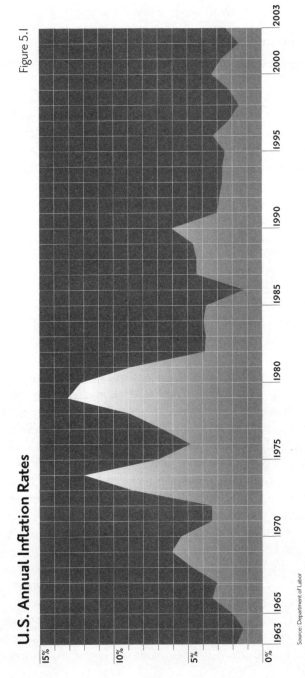

U.S. Annual Inflation Rates

Figure 5.1

Source: Department of Labor

more later. (2) You should always borrow to buy (the use of OPM—"other people's money"). (3) You can never accumulate enough. (4) The rate of inflation is standard for everyone. These myths have just enough truth in them to make them believable, and many people govern their economic lives by them.

Several years ago a man came into my office, and as we were discussing his financial situation, he made a startling statement: "I sure wish we would go back to double-digit inflation." I was surprised and asked him to explain what he meant. He said that during the early 1980s he had been earning 18 percent, 19 percent, and 20 percent on the money he had invested in a money market fund. However, since the inflation rate had been reduced, he was earning substantially less on his investment. He had never made so much money as when we had double-digit inflation!

His statement was exactly right, and his experience is the experience of history. During times of inflation, the magic of compounding can either work for you or against you, depending on whether you are borrowing money (negative compounding) or lending money as an investor (positive compounding). When I discussed this with a banker friend, he described a study done by some Swiss bankers. Their study showed that over the last seven hundred years, the average annual rate of interest charged for loans was approximately 3 percent greater than the average annual inflation rate. So, the real rate of return to the lender was 3 percent, not the 5 percent, 10 percent, 12 percent, and the like that they actually charged. If this is true, then everyone lending money (which we do when we put money into any kind of savings fund) should be able to average, over the long run, at least 3 percent more than the inflation rate. This is extremely important because, if it is true, by being on the lending side of inflation, you will have the magic of compounding working for you, and you will *always beat inflation*. No longer is it something to be feared!

I am not advocating inflation, because in the long run it destroys a currency and undermines the economic and political system. However, if we are destined to have inflation, it should at the very least work for us rather than against us.

The fact that the interest earned will be taxed does make a significant difference in how much can ultimately be accumulated. For example, $2,000 per year invested in something that is either tax-exempt or tax deferred, such as an IRA that yields 12 percent per year, will grow to $144,104 in twenty years and $1,534,182 in forty years, whereas the same amount invested to yield 8 percent after tax (a 33 percent combined tax rate) will grow to $91,424 in twenty years and only $518,112 in forty years—over $1,000,000 less over forty years, just because of the taxes paid on the earnings each year.

The important point is the "real interest rate," not the stated rate. Historically, the real interest rate has beaten inflation by 3 percent, but taxes can destroy this spread unless taxes and income are indexed for inflation. This is exactly what happens in countries that experience high inflation rates, and it has already happened in our country.

Understanding the magic of compounding, the concept of margin, and the *real* interest rates prepares us to deal with the myths of inflation. We must also remember that God is sovereign and can impose His will into any personal financial situation or political system.

Myth 1: Buy Now Because It Will Cost More Later

This statement appears to make good financial sense at first reading, but it presupposes that in the future you absolutely will need the item you are buying. The real question then is not what it costs or what it will cost, but rather, do you need it? The myth encourages us to delude ourselves into funding our *greeds* rather than our *needs*. Advertisers really play on this myth by advertising that next year the cost is going to go up. So what? God has obligated Himself to meet my needs always (see Philippians 4:19), and He didn't qualify that by saying "except for times of inflation."

The second thing that this myth presupposes, of course, is an increasing price; but there is example after example after example of the fallacy of sure increases, even during times of inflation. Ask any farmer how much his land has appreciated over the last few years. Yet just a few years ago, "everyone" knew that farmland would always go up because there is a limited supply of it. How about the price of clothes? Or what about the price of computers and electronic equipment? Or how about long-distance telephone rates? Or what about mortgage rates? Those who purchased and mortgaged homes in 1983 at a 14 percent or 15 percent fixed rate because the rates would never go down have probably refinanced at least once or twice in the recent years.

Be wary of the trap of buying anything because the price is going up in the future. First of all, ask yourself, "Do I really need this?" Second, ask, "If I do, but can't afford it, has God promised to meet my needs?" Of course He has, but not necessarily until you *really have a need* and not for the finest, most costly merchandise when something more affordable will do. He never seems to meet my needs in advance, but always right on time. My late friend Larry Burkett often said, "God is seldom early, but never late."

If you decide to fund your *greeds* now because of the possibility of future price increases, my advice is to do so with cash and never with borrowed money. Paying cash will cause you to make a better decision, and at least you will not have compounding working against you. You do, of course, experience the "opportunity cost of consumption" described in the last chapter.

Myth 2: Always Borrow to Buy

Two elements of truth support this myth: first, in times of inflation, the loan is paid back in cheaper dollars than those borrowed (because of the decline in purchasing power); and second, the tax deduction for interest expense reduces the cost of interest.

However, the myth has two presuppositions:

1. It presupposes a rate of interest that is less than the inflation rate, and a purchase that appreciates or earns more than the after-tax cost. In other words, it makes economic sense.

2. The cash or investment that could be used for the purchase is earning more than the cost of borrowing. Again, borrowing in that case makes economic sense.

These presuppositions are generally either ignored or not known. The guiding principle now seems to be: Always borrow because you need the interest expense for a tax deduction, and you will always be paying back with cheaper dollars.

To borrow money for the tax deduction is foolish. If you are in the 25 percent tax bracket, for every $100 spent on interest, you reduce your taxes by $25, *but* it costs you $100 to do so; therefore, you are out of pocket $75 ($100–$25). Spending more than what you save is hardly the way to achieve financial success, and yet this advice is given regularly, even by professionals who should know better.

It is true that in times of inflation you will be paying back borrowed dollars that are worth less than when you borrowed them. However, if you used the borrowed dollars to buy anything that depreciates in value, you have gained nothing financially by doing so and may have even lost in the whole transaction.

In recent years with lower inflation, I hear less of these arguments for debt financing during inflationary times. But these myths die hard. My point is that always borrowing to buy just because of inflation ignores the presuppositions mentioned above. Using debt during times of inflation for leverage purposes can make sense, *but* only if these presuppositions are not ignored. In the next chapter we will take a close look at the leverage issue and the way leveraging has been distorted to justify funding whatever we want.

Myth 3: You Can Never Accumulate Enough

Understanding real interest rates and the magic of compounding is the key to destroying the myth that you can never accumulate enough to be protected from inflation during times of inflation. Incidentally, this myth is not a myth during times of hyperinflation if *all* of your assets are invested in money market instruments. (See chapter 10 for how to protect yourself against this threat.)

First of all, this myth raises the question, what is "enough"? In my opinion, to accumulate enough means that I must have enough in an investment fund at retirement to generate enough income to live, give, and pay taxes. In other words, that investment fund must have sufficient "earning power" to provide for your lifetime.

In times of inflation, the earning power of investment funds will, over time, always be greater than the inflation rate, unless the investor ties his or her money up at a fixed rate of interest for a long-term—which is foolishness in times of inflation.

A wise and knowledgeable person can beat inflation by spending less than is earned, because the earning power of money will, over time, always be greater than the inflation rate. That earning power will even offset the required increase in income needed just to maintain a standard of living.

The myth that you can never accumulate enough prevails because there are many variables that enter in:

- ❖ Time or the number of years until retirement
- ❖ The short-term goals, excluding children, accumulation needs, and mortgage payments. In other words, what could you live on if you did not have children to support, a mortgage payment, or the need to save?
- ❖ Additional income from other sources at retirement
- ❖ The inflation rate
- ❖ The after-tax yield now and in the future
- ❖ Your current cash-flow margin
- ❖ Current amount of investment funds
- ❖ Your personal inflation rate

The effect of these variables may be seen in the formula below:

Providing for Retirement

Illustration 5.1

1. Years until retirement	25
2. Estimated short-term goals need	$25,000
3. Less: Retirement income	$(12,500)
Annual amount needed	$12,500
4. Inflation factor	6%
Future income needed annually (from chart 5-A)	$53,625
5. Assumed after-tax yield on investments ÷	10%
Investment fund needed	$536,250
6. Current investment fund	$25,000
Amount it will grow to (from chart 4-B)	$(270,867)
Unfunded investment need	$265,383
7. Annual cash-flow margin needed to invest (from chart 4-C)	$2,453

The illustration assumes several things: The retirement income received from other sources will grow at least at the inflation rate; the ability to invest at after-tax yields will be considerably greater than the inflation rate; and the rate of inflation will not reach the level of hyperinflation. The illustration also ignores the impact of inflation on the investment fund at retirement when the entire yield, which had been compounding, is being used to live on. Therefore, the "investment fund needed" is a minimum amount. The point is that if you are spending less than you earn, inflation can work for you rather than against you and you can fund enough. Even if you do not see how, God is still responsible to meet your needs and only requires that you take the first step of faith and obedience. In this case, that step is to generate a positive cash-flow margin.

Myth 4: The Rate of Inflation Is Standard for Everyone

In personal financial planning, we figure for the impact of inflation by using the reported inflation rate. However, the reported national rate of inflation is an average and assumes that one makes significant purchases, such as a home, monthly. Such things just don't happen.

It has been my experience that when couples who plan to have a cash-flow margin do so by living on some type of workable and simple budget, their personal rate of inflation is substantially less than the reported rate. They know what they spend and become price sensitive so that they are not victimized by inflation. On the other hand, if they have expenses over which they have no control, at the very least, they know how to pray specifically for God's intervention in the sure faith that God has committed to meet their needs.

The Impact of Inflation on Retirement — Illustration 5.2

1. Years until retirement	25
2. Estimated short-term goals need	$25,000
3. Less: Retirement income	$(12,500)
Annual amount needed	$12,500
4. Personal inflation factor	2%
Future income needed annually (from chart 5-A)	$20,500
5. Assumed after-tax yield on investment ÷	10%
Investment fund needed	$205,000
6. Current investment fund	$25,000
Amount it will grow to (from chart 4-B)	$(270,867)
Unfunded (Overfunded) investment fund	$(65,867)
7. Annual cash-flow margin needed	$-0-

To see the tremendous impact of a personal inflation rate that is less than the reported average annual inflation rate, assume that in our previous illustration the personal inflation factor is only 2 percent rather than the 6 percent national average.

The current investment fund grows to more than enough to meet the future income needs with *no* cash-flow margin needed for the next twenty-five years to meet regular living expenses. Of course, if this family lives in such a disciplined way that they have a cash-flow margin, they can save for long-term goals, such as major giving.

The following formula is for your own personal example:

Your Retirement Worksheet

Illustration 5.3

1. Years until retirement		
2. Estimated short-term goals need	$	
3. Less: Retirement income	$(	)
Annual amount needed	$	
4. Personal inflation factor		%
Future income needed annually (from chart 5-A)	$	
5. Assumed after-tax yield on investment ÷		%
Investment fund needed	$	
6. Current investment fund	$	
Amount it will grow to (from chart 4-B)	$(	)
Unfunded (Overfunded) investment fund	$	
7. Annual cash-flow margin needed (from chart 4-C)	$	

Conclusion

Inflation does not necessarily need to be feared. For those who are wise, knowledgeable, patient, self-disciplined, and mature, it can work to their advantage.

In the last chapter, we raised the question of how much various compounded amounts would be worth in forty years. Let's assume you had $75,000 in your retirement plan. In this chapter we implied that if we had a substantial level of inflation, your money could end up with substantially more than $75,000 because the "real interest rate" will always be greater than the inflation rate. In other words, as inflation rises, so do interest rates. So if inflation increases during the last few years of your investing, your investment would be more than $75,000 upon withdrawal. To get that $75,000, we were assuming a constant interest rate.

We also demonstrated that the "earning power" of that $75,000 would be more than enough to provide for retirement. If your life expectancy were thirty years beyond retirement, $75,000 would provide $2,500 per year if you withdrew it all at once the first year of your retirement. If you withdraw little by little, each year, you will earn back a significant amount in interest again.

If you are a lender and an investor of money rather than a borrower of money, you can likely beat inflation. In the next chapter we will look at the foolishness and devastation of being a borrower of money.

THE DANGERS OF DEBT

> *"He that goes a borrowing goes a sorrowing."*
> BENJAMIN FRANKLIN
>
> *"A bank is a place that will lend you money if you can prove that you don't need it."*
> BOB HOPE
>
> *"When a man is in love or in debt, someone else has the advantage."*
> BILL BALNCE
>
> *"Neither a borrower nor a lender be;*
> *For loan oft loses both itself and friend,*
> *And borrowing dulls the edge of husbandry."*
> WILLIAM SHAKESPEARE, *HAMLET*, ACT 1: SCENE 3

The financial topic of debt is clouded with emotion, misunderstanding, and poor teaching. Before starting, we need to have a clear understanding of debt.

- ❖ Debt is not a sin! The Bible discourages the use of debt, but does not prohibit it.

- ❖ Debt is never the real problem; it is only symptomatic of real problems—greed, self-indulgence, impatience, fear, poor self-image, lack of self-worth, lack of self-discipline, and perhaps many others.

- ❖ Debt can be defined many ways. I define it as *any money owed to anyone for anything.*

There are five different kinds of debt: (1) credit card debt, (2) consumer debt, (3) mortgage debt, (4) investment debt, and (5) business debt.

In using any of the five kinds of debts, there are always four questions to ask:

1. Does it make economic sense?

2. Do my spouse and I have unity about taking on this debt?

3. Do I have the spiritual peace of mind or freedom to enter into this debt?

4. What personal goals and values am I meeting with this debt that can be met in *no* other way?

Economic Dangers of Debt

The primary economic danger of debt is that compounding works against you rather than for you. For example, a thirty-year mortgage on a home at 7 percent interest requires that you pay back nearly two and one-half times the original amount borrowed.

Borrowed	$100,000
Interest rate	7%
Monthly payment	665.30
Months paid	X 360
TOTAL PAYMENTS	**$239,508**

Or, to use a car loan illustration, assume the following:

New car cost	$25,000
Interest rate	9%
Monthly payment	518.96
Months paid	X 60
TOTAL PAYMENTS	**$31,138**

Now if you purchase another car in five years and again finance it and continue to do this over a working life of forty years, you will have purchased eight cars and paid in car payments $31,138 x 8 = $249,104. The bank received $518.96 per month for 480 months and never had at risk any more than $25,000; they in turn reinvested that $518.96 in other loans yielding 9 percent, so that they accumulated over $2.4 million on your total payments of $249,104. What if, instead of making car payments, you paid yourself $518.96 per month and were able to invest that payment at 9 percent? Then *you* would have the $2.4 million, not the lending institution! The true cost of driving those cars is $2.4 million, not $249,104 in total payments.

Don't get me wrong. I am not against buying a new car, nor do I believe bankers are dishonest. (As a matter of fact, I used to own a major interest in two small banks.) But I am pointing out that consumption has a higher cost than many have ever realized. In chapter 9, I will outline for you the most economical way to buy that new car, because many of us, myself included, enjoy driving a new car.

The second economic danger of debt is that debt becomes a trap—getting in takes no effort, but getting out can be next to impossible. In many cases, borrowing money can be no more difficult than signing your name or, at the most, filling out a lengthy form. Even borrowing the initial money for investments or starting a business can be almost effortless. It's so easy. It's like finding money lying on the street. It gives a great feeling of satisfaction and power, at least momentarily. Then it turns and uses its power as a stranglehold on you!

Ease of Debt Growth

Chart 6-A

YEARS	OVERSPENDING	TOTAL DEBT	INTEREST PAID
1	$1,000	$1,000	$100
2	1,000	2,000	200
3	1,000	3,000	300
4	1,000	4,000	400
5	1,000	5,000	500
6	1,000	6,000	600
7	1,000	7,000	700
8	1,000	8,000	800
9	1,000	9,000	900
10	1,000	10,000	1,000
TOTAL	$10,000		$5,500

The realization of the trap comes when the borrowed money must be paid back, because by then the glamour has worn off whatever was purchased, and the money used to repay the debt takes away the opportunity to buy other things. For example, assume that a couple overspends their income $1,000 each year for ten years on impulsive purchases. Then realizing that they are $10,000 in debt, they decide to begin a program to get out of debt. By this point, not only are they overspending by $1,000 each year, but they are also paying at least $1,000 per year in pure interest (if the interest rate is only 10 percent). Plus, another $1,000 for debt repayment on the actual cost of the items, which have long since become old, broken, and almost despised because of the resentment of paying for them.

Debt Repayment

Chart 6-B

YEARS	DEBT REPAYMENT	TOTAL DEBT	INTEREST PAID
11	$1,000	$9,000	$1,000
12	1,000	8,000	900
13	1,000	7,000	800
14	1,000	6,000	700
15	1,000	5,000	600
16	1,000	4,000	500
17	1,000	3,000	400
18	1,000	2,000	300
19	1,000	1,000	200
20	1,000	-0-	100
TOTAL	$10,000		$5,500

When they decide to get out of debt, first of all they must stop going into debt. Second, they must begin to pay back the accumulated debt and, all the while, continue to pay the interest. Their real costs are shown below.

Their total cost to overspend by $10,000 ($1,000 per year for ten years) is $31,000. Notice that when they made their decision to get out of debt in year ten, their only cost was $1,000 per year in interest, but immediately after their decision in year eleven, the effective cost went to $3,000, because they must forego in years eleven through twenty overspending formerly done in years one through ten. Just think—$21,000 that could have been used in far more productive and fun ways!

True Cost of Debt

Chart 6-C

YEARS	OVERSPENDING REDUCTION	TOTAL DEBT	INTEREST PAID	TOTAL COST
1	0	0	$100	$100
2	0	0	200	200
3	0	0	300	300
4	0	0	400	400
5	0	0	500	500
6	0	0	600	600
7	0	0	700	700
8	0	0	800	800
9	0	0	900	900
10	0	0	1,000	1,000
11	$1,000	$1,000	1,000	3,000
12	1,000	1,000	900	2,900
13	1,000	1,000	800	2,800
14	1,000	1,000	700	2,700
15	1,000	1,000	600	2,600
16	1,000	1,000	500	2,500
17	1,000	1,000	400	2,400
18	1,000	1,000	300	2,300
19	1,000	1,000	200	2,200
20	1,000	1,000	100	2,100
TOTAL	$10,000	$10,000	$11,000	$31,000

In chapter 3, I said that financial maturity is "giving up today's desires for future benefits." Also, the longer term the perspective, the better the financial decision is likely to be. Chart 6-C dramatically depicts these two principles.

There is another cost which is not so apparent; that is the income tax consequences. For example, in year eleven, not only must they earn the $3,000 cost, but they must also earn the taxes on that $3,000 in order to have $3,000 left to pay the lender.

Income	$4,000
Taxes at 25%	$1,000
Balance available	$3,000

They must earn $4,000 in order to have $3,000 left. For most debt, the interest costs are not deductible.

The third economic danger to debt is that *debt always mortgages the future.* With debt, the first priority use of future income must be debt repayment—not giving or lifestyle or investing or even taxes! The freedom of choice disappears.

The consequences of debt are a paradox. Current marketplace wisdom says to you, "Raise your standard of living by buying what you want and pay for it while you enjoy it," but the reality is that you may be sentencing yourself to a lower standard of living in the future. Look again at chart 6-C.

This couple enjoyed themselves to the tune of $1,000 per year beyond their income in the first ten years, but their second ten years was being mortgaged and resulted in a *much* greater cost than the earlier benefit. The paradox is that while seeming to raise their standard of living, they were in reality, over the long term, lowering it. What a deception! This illustration may portray why so many couples go through some very difficult times or divorce after eight to twelve years of marriage.

Spiritual Dangers of Debt

Two spiritual dangers of borrowing money exist. First, borrowing *always* presumes upon the future, and second, borrowing *may* deny God an opportunity to work.

The Bible definitely warns us about presuming upon the future. In James 4:16, presuming upon the future is called "arrogance." In Luke 14:28, Jesus said: "For which of you, intending to build a tower, does not sit down first and count the cost, whether he has enough to finish it?" Whenever any money is borrowed for any purpose, there is a presumption of repayment. In fact, from the lender's viewpoint it is not only a presumption, it is a certainty.

A friend and I were discussing the biblical admonition against presuming upon the future and the requirement that whenever a Christian borrows money it must be paid back. Psalm 37:21 says in part, "The wicked borrows and does not repay." We concluded that many Christians in America might be counting on the Rapture to get them out of debt. He said to me, "Wouldn't it be something if, when Jesus came back to rapture the church, He left all the Christians who had debt of any kind here on earth to repay it rather than taking them to heaven?" Both of us became quiet, and then he said jokingly, "You know, maybe the Rapture has already occurred!"

An important biblical financial principle flows out of that truth:

◇◇

Whenever you borrow money for any reason, there must be a guaranteed way to pay it back.

◇◇

Not a "hoped-for" way, such as an increase in income, nor even the continuation of income, but there must be a guaranteed way *regardless* of the circumstances. If this principle were followed, there would be almost no risk to debt. Not to have a guaranteed way to repay is *always* to presume upon the future.

The second spiritual danger of debt is that it *may* deny God an opportunity to work. Over the years I have started several businesses of my own and have had the privilege of counseling many hundreds of others who have been in the initial stages of founding their own businesses. One of the things that is standard in starting a business is to secure from a bank a line of credit or some terms of financing so there is always cash available to meet the unexpected needs of a new business. Therefore, when I started a financial planning business in the fall of 1979, I went to the bank and arranged for a line of credit.

In the following weeks, as I prayed through the many issues regarding the starting of this business, I felt less and less comfortable with having borrowed to start this business, even though it made "good sense." Eventually, I felt so strongly convicted about the need not to have debt that I called the bank and canceled my line of credit. This was an extremely risky thing to do, as I had a totally unproven business, no clients, and very little financial resources personally.

Approximately one week after I canceled the line of credit, I was visiting in the training department of a major international corporation headquartered in Atlanta. During the conversation with one of the training directors, he asked me if I had any interest in developing a financial planning seminar for his organization. As a matter of fact, I had been in the process at that very time of developing a financial planning seminar in order to provide a conceptual framework for the financial planning process. Of course I said, "Yes." He then asked me how much I would charge them to develop such a seminar. I had no idea what large corporations paid for such work, so I simply asked, "What would you pay?"

He thought for a moment before saying they would pay me $6,000 to develop the seminar and another $4,000 if I would teach it four times during the next year—a total of $10,000. Coincidentally, the line of credit I had arranged at the bank was for $10,000. Of course, I replied that $10,000 for that work sounded "very fair." He also asked me if they could go ahead and pay me the $6,000 immediately in order to get it into the current year's budget. With no hesitation I gave him my address.

I am convinced that had I not canceled the line of credit with the bank and depended solely upon God to provide the resources, I never would have received the contract to design the seminar. I am convinced that had I borrowed the money, the training director would never have made the offer he did, because to this day I can take no credit for having pursued the money. God provided it in an unusual, undeniable, and supernatural fashion!

In many cases, when we borrow the money to fund one item, be it for the purpose of a new car, a television, a new home, a vacation, or whatever, we are putting the lender in the place of God. Who needs God to provide for us if someone will lend to us?

We seem to be very unwilling to wait for God's timing and for God's method to meet our needs and our desires. We prefer to have it done our way, in our timing. Yet Isaiah 55:8-9 says, "'For my thoughts are not your thoughts, neither are your ways my ways,' declares the LORD. 'As the heavens are higher than the earth, so are my ways higher than your ways and my thoughts than your thoughts.'" Invariably, God's method of meeting my needs and desires is different from my method. The question that we need to ask ourselves is, does God provide for what I want by providing borrowed funds, or is this me—meeting my needs and desires in my own way and timing?

Biblical Principles of Borrowing

In addition to presuming upon the future and potentially denying God an opportunity to work, there are many other biblical principles relative to debt and borrowing. In Psalm 37:21 we read, "The wicked borrow and do not repay, but the righteous give generously." The principle that comes from this verse is that not repaying debt is never an option for the Christian. This verse also implies that a righteous person is able to give rather than borrow. I personally do not believe that financial success is necessarily symptomatic of righteousness. If we equate righteousness and financial success, many evil people could be defined as righteous. All of us have seen too many examples to the contrary. Yet I do feel strongly that if we are Christians in action as well as in name, then we will aim to reach the mark to become debt free. That way we can have a lifestyle of giving without hesitation or fear when the Lord lays upon our heart to do so.

Romans 13:8 says, "Let no debt remain outstanding, except the continuing debt to love one another, for he who loves his fellowman has fulfilled the law." The context of this passage does not deal with finances. (Even if it were on finances, I do not believe that it specifically prohibits debt.) What it does do, however, is set up a principle that says, "If I owe anyone anything, I am not free to give love to that person." Anyone who has borrowed money from another person, and especially another Christian, realizes the wall that immediately goes up from being in a debtor/lender relationship. Debtors and lenders are not really free to love one another. This verse suggests principles for both sides. Lending to another Christian needs to be considered very, very seriously before it is done. On the other side, before you borrow from anyone for anything, consider the ramifications of being in bondage to that person. Are you, in fact, free to love that person if you owe him something?

Proverbs 22:7 says, "The rich rule over the poor, and the borrower is servant to the lender." Anyone who has borrowed or been in bondage to debt knows the truth of this verse. The reality is that whenever you have borrowed from anyone, you are a servant to that person. This verse does not prohibit debt, of course, but it certainly cautions against the use of debt. We could say that anyone who uses debt for any purpose, at the very least, is not using biblical wisdom and, in fact, may be a "fool." Again, this is a wise caution but not a prohibition against debt.

First Timothy 5:8 says, "If anyone does not provide for his relatives, and especially for his immediate family, he has denied the faith and is worse than an unbeliever." The underlying biblical principle relative to debt in this verse is that by taking on debt you may run the risk of not providing for your own. Because debt mortgages the future and because the negative compounding of debt works against you, you may very well end up in the future not being able to provide for your own. Debt by its nature assumes that our financial situation will stay the same or improve, when that may not necessarily be

God's plan. Therefore, this verse says that you have denied the faith and are worse than an unbeliever. Obviously, the danger of debt is great and needs to be avoided.

Luke 12:15 says, "Then [Jesus] said to them, 'Watch out! Be on your guard against all kinds of greed; a man's life does not consist in the abundance of his possessions.'" The caution in this verse is clear: Beware and be on your guard against every form of greed and guard against relying on **things** for your sense of worth and accomplishment. Debt makes it very easy to fund greeds; yet in doing so, we may violate the biblical principle set forth in this verse. The question to ask is, am I funding my needs or my greeds?

Another absolute biblical principle is to avoid surety. In the book of Proverbs much is said about "surety" and the foolishness of it (Proverbs 22:26–27). Surety itself is not debt, but it is rather guaranteeing the debt of another. To be a surety on any debt is violation of a definite biblical principle. Many people equate surety and debt, and they are the same in the sense that both are obligations to debt and repayment. But debt is personal in nature (you take on the amount you know you can afford and still provide for your family). Surety obligates you and your family to *another* person's debt regardless of their abilities, morality, and responsibility (or lack of it). There is a difference in the two.

The Bible contains many other passages dealing with money and specifically with debt. Why is so much written about debt in God's Word? I believe there are three reasons. First of all, debt is extremely deceptive. As we said earlier, getting into debt is easy, and God knew that all humans could be attracted to it, so He had to sound loud warnings against it. Getting out of debt is next to impossible. Second, debt creates bondage, and if that bondage is to the world system, we are no longer free to be the witnesses in this world that God has called us to be. Third, debt is blasphemous when we rely on it and deny God an opportunity to work. With all of these cautions and warnings against debt, I still believe that in some cases debt is acceptable, but only under certain conditions.

Criteria for Undertaking Any Debt

Here are four criteria that may help you determine if taking on a debt is acceptable.

First of all, does it make economic sense to incur the debt? To determine this, there are two rules to follow:

❖ The cost to borrow (after-tax interest) must be *less than* the economic benefit received (interest, yield, and/or growth in value).

❖ There must be a *guaranteed* way of repayment.

Second, are *both* spouses free from any anxiety regarding this debt? This criteria indicates that there must be absolute unity between the spouses.

Third, can the debt be undertaken with spiritual peace of mind? The rule is that if I experience any lack of peace when I picture myself taking on this debt, I do not enter into the debt.

Fourth, I ask myself, "What 'God-given' goals and objectives am I meeting with this debt that can be met in *no* other way?"

I believe these criteria are practical, pragmatic, and biblical and should be applied unemotionally to every debt opportunity. They leave us with the following conclusions as we apply them to the five kinds of debt:

1. *Credit card debt.* I define credit card debt as carrying a balance, or paying finance charges, on the credit card debt owed. Paying off your entire balance every month does not result in credit card debt. The problem is not the use of credit cards, but the abuse of them. Credit card debt will never satisfy the economic criteria and, therefore, should never be used. Using credit card debt, which always has a high interest rate, to accumulate the consumptive and depreciating items makes no sense economically. Whether or not to use credit cards for convenience will be addressed in chapter 9.

2. *Consumer debt.* Consumer debt is debt that is used to finance cars, furniture, vacations, and other consumptive and depreciating items. It is exactly like credit card debt except that the process of applying for it can be more lengthy. Because it is just like credit card debt, it should be avoided at all costs.

Both credit card debt and consumer debt are to be avoided, I believe, not because they are sinful in themselves, unless they are being used to satisfy greed (see Luke 12:15), but because they just don't make sense economically. The only exception (and I do *not* have an example or illustration of this) would be using them for a personal goal and value that could be met in no other way, a personal goal and value that unquestionably came from God. Implicitly, this says that God has chosen debt to meet a personal need. Again, I have never seen an example of this, but I would not want to put God into a box and say that He could never do it.

3. *Mortgage debt.* We Americans have come to believe that owning a home is a God-given right. Our children expect to begin their married life in a home it took our parents a lifetime to save for! Additionally, during the last generation, especially the years 1960 to 1980, a home purchased with a fixed interest rate was the safest and surest way to build personal net worth and equity. However, the "rules of the game" changed. In the 1980s and 1990s, when housing prices softened in some regions of the country and inflation slowed dramatically, it has taken a while for our society to recognize this, and I don't believe we have, as yet, accepted that housing price increases are a "sure thing."

When considering the purchase of a home, we should apply the same four criteria as for undertaking any debt. However, the economic criteria are very difficult to nail down in today's economic environment. Even in the period 1960 to 1980, there was not a guaranteed way to pay the debt except for returning the home back to the lending institution. My counsel to young couples who are considering the purchase of a home is never to become so attached to the home that they could not give it up if the debt could not be paid. Jobs are not nearly as secure today as they were in the past.

The psychological burden of home mortgage debt is more severe than most people think, especially if the wife has her center of influence and security in her home. Studies have shown that having mortgage debt is a stressful factor and that the degree of stress relates to the amount of the mortgage.

The question of whether or not to pay off the mortgage, if that is an option, is really an economic, psychological, and spiritual decision. Economically, it may not make sense to pay off a low-interest-rate mortgage, even if one has the funds to do so. However, psychologically and spiritually, it may be, by far, the best course. Again, I would remind you that money is nothing more than a resource to accomplish other goals and objectives—it is never an end in itself. Therefore, even if it does not make economic sense to pay off a mortgage, there may be higher priority goals and objectives to be met. Money then becomes merely the resource to meet those goals. The decision does not have to always be an economic one. That counsel is, of course, applicable to all decisions.

4. *Investment and business debt.* The order of applying the four basic criteria for any debt is a good one before taking on investment or business debt. Let me repeat the criteria here: Is the rate of return greater than the cost, both on an after-tax basis? Is there a guaranteed way to repay the debt? Are both spouses in perfect agreement and unity? And do you have spiritual peace of mind when considering this debt?

Vulnerability of Stress Scale

Psychiatrist Thomas H. Holmes and his colleagues at the University of Washington School of Medicine have developed a scale to measure the relative stress induced by various changes in a person's life. The amount of stress is measured on a point scale of two hundred "life-change units." Studies by Dr. Holmes and his associates show that if you accumulate more than three hundred units in a single year, your life has probably been disrupted enough to make you vulnerable to illness.

Stress Producers   Illustration 6.1

EVENT	SCALE OF IMPACT
Death of spouse	100
Divorce	73
Marital separation	65
Jail term	63
Death of close family member	63
Personal injury or illness	53
Marriage	50
Fired at work	47
Marital reconciliation	45
Retirement	45
Change in health of a family member	44
Pregnancy	40
Sex difficulties	39
Gain of new family member	39

Business readjustment	39
Change in financial state	38
Death of close friend	37
Change to different line of work	36
Change in number of arguments with spouse	35
Loan over $10,000	31
Foreclosure of mortgage or loan	30
Change in responsibilities at work	29
Son or daughter leaving home	29
Trouble with in-laws	29
Outstanding personal achievement	28
Wife begins or stops work	26
Begin or end school	26
Change in living conditions	25
Revision of personal habits	24
Trouble with boss	23
Change in work hours or conditions	20
Change in residence	20
Change in recreation	19
Change in church activities	19
Change in social activities	18
Loan less than $10,000	17
Change in sleeping habits	16
Change in number of family get-togethers	15
Change in eating habits	15
Vacation	13
Christmas	12
Minor violation of the law	11

My experience has been that no business opportunity or invest-ment opportunity ever comes packaged as anything other than "a good deal." I probably see a thousand so-called "good deals" a year. No one has ever come to the office or sent a proposal and said, "Let me show you a bad deal." On the front end, every business and in-vestment deal is a good one. It only went bad later! What makes them so difficult to evaluate and reject is that they are all presented as good deals, which a person would be foolish to turn down. There-fore, there never seems to be economic justification alone for turning them down.

This is one of the reasons I feel it is so important to apply the rule that a husband and wife have perfect unity on their debt decisions.

I remember speaking one time to a group of professional athletes, and as I related that rule with them, one of the wives sat with tears streaming down her cheeks. Afterward she shared with me how her husband, who had played on three Super Bowl championship teams, had been presented with a business opportunity that was a "sure thing." Against his wife's counsel, he had mortgaged everything, gone into the business, and had eventually lost all they owned. What does a forty-year-old ex-athlete with no training or money and a family do? It was a tragic, yet typical, case.

I give two general rules in this area. First of all, if you cannot explain the deal or investment to your spouse in such a way that he or she totally understands it, don't do it. Second, even if you can explain it so that your spouse totally understands it, but he or she feels uneasy or unsure in any way about it, don't do it. Granted, you may pass up many opportunities. However, one of the surest ways to financial success is to avoid major mistakes, because not only do you have to make up for the lost investment, but you also lose the earnings that this money could have generated, and the earnings that the earnings could have generated, and the earnings that the earnings that the earnings could have generated. Again, the biblical counsel is sound: "He who gathers money little by little makes it grow." Or as we stated in chapter 4, "Get rich slowly."

Many times one spouse has a God-given intuition, has common-sense discomfort, or sees loopholes in the deal. The more enthusiastic spouse understandably wouldn't have these if it were his idea. None of us want to be told "No" or have water thrown on our ideas. But God gives us one another for help, protection, and comfort. Take time to honestly think through and listen to a spouse's point of view. Come to absolute agreement and willingness to mentally and emotionally "let go" of the money, because that is always a possibility.

You also want to guard against the blame game in the future. If a spouse disagrees, she has every right to say, "I told you so." The temptation for resentment and division in your marriage is too great if there is disagreement. No amount of monetary return can replace trust and unity between you and your spouse. No amount of ego-boost resulting from a "great" investment and from doing things your way "no matter what he or she says" is worth breaking the heart of your spouse. You communicate value to your spouse by asking and waiting for his agreement in financial matters. You communicate control and carelessness by forging ahead against her wishes. Consider this: Perhaps a spouse is not trying to squelch your hopes and dreams of financial success; perhaps he or she is protecting them, because they can foresee problems in the plan.

Again, let me say, debt is not a sin. The Bible discourages the use of debt, but does not prohibit it. *Being in debt is never the real problem; it is only symptomatic of the real problem.* The real problem is usually greed, self-indulgence, impatience, fear, a poor self-image, or lack of self-discipline. So, if you find yourself in debt, your first question is not, how do I get out of debt? Ask first of all, "Why am I in this situation?" and answer that question. Then the next step to getting out of debt is, first of all, to stop going into debt, and then second, to set up some type of repayment plan.

Please understand that I am not being judgmental. Through years of teaching and counseling I know better than most the temptation that debt presents. My heart goes out to the many young couples, and even older couples, whom I have visited and who will suffer under the burden of debt for many years to come. But they must recognize the problem that caused the debt and then, as Proverbs 3:5–6 says, "Trust in the LORD with all your heart, and lean not on your own understanding; in all your ways acknowledge Him, and He shall direct your paths." God is faithful and will provide a way.

7

WHERE AM I?

*"Some couples go over their budgets very carefully every month;
others just go over them."*
SALLY POPLIN

*"Even if you're on the right track, you'll get run over
if you just sit there."*
WILL ROGERS

*"Be sure you know the condition of your flocks,
give careful attention to your herds."*
PROVERBS 27:23

W e have looked at many principles and concepts. We have defined stewardship as "the use of God-given resources for the accomplishment of God-given goals," and as "the allocation of limited resources to unlimited alternatives." We have also reviewed the magic of compounding and concluded that a dollar spent today takes multiple dollars out of the future, while a dollar saved today puts multiple dollars into the future.

We then looked at the concept of cash-flow margin and concluded that there was only one way to achieve financial freedom and success, and that was to spend less than you earn and do it over a long time period. In the last chapter, we examined the kinds of debt and the four criteria to apply before taking on debt. Now we are ready to put these principles and concepts into practical application—to answer the question, where am I?

When I ask others how they are doing financially, they typically respond by telling me what their income is or by telling me about their most recent expensive purchase. In reality, neither may be of importance in describing financial health. To know conclusively where you are financially is necessary before you can even begin to plan for the accomplishment of goals, dreams, and desires.

The Financial Planning Diagram on page 81 depicts four steps to financial planning.

Step 1: "Summarize Present Situation" will be covered in this chapter and basically answers the question, where am I?

Step 2: "Establish Financial Goals" will be covered in the next chapter and answers the question, where do I want to go?

Steps 3 and *4:* "Increase Cash-Flow Margin" and "Control Cash Flow" answer the question, how do I get to where I want to go from where I am? They will be covered in chapters 9 through 13.

Before you move from step 1 to step 2, you need to analyze where you are relative to where you want to go. Three financial summaries will give you the necessary facts concerning your current standing:

❖ Statement of net worth

❖ Summary of cash flow

❖ Summary of life insurance coverage

Statement of Net Worth

A statement of net worth is much like a snapshot or x-ray. It summarizes those financial transactions at a specific point in time. This summary reflects every financial decision that has been made up to that point in time. Specifically, a statement of net worth lists all of the assets that are owned, then subtracts from that listing of assets all of the liabilities, or debts, owed. The resulting number totals one's net worth.

Over time, children often learn that by performing odd jobs or working part-time or full-time jobs they can earn money. For the most part, that money is spent on personal needs and desires and, therefore, the accumulation is not very great; but at least there is some accumulation.

In typical fashion, after high school or college, young people go to work and find that their income does not support their needs. Therefore, they borrow to fund some of their desires and needs—an automobile, some furniture, a home, and maybe even further education. If they add up what they have accumulated in the way of cash, investments, furniture, cars, and homes, they will have the total of all they own. However, they may have a substantial amount of debt which, when subtracted from what they own, would leave a small or even a negative net worth situation.

Financial Planning Diagram

Figure 7.1

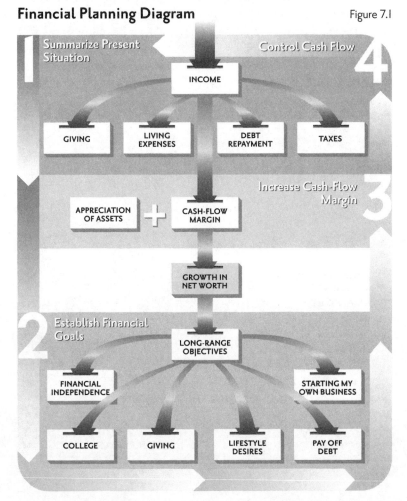

At any point anyone can add up his or her assets, subtract liabilities, and get a picture of the net worth. This one number is the net result of every previous financial decision. An increasing net worth means that your assets are increasing more than your debts.

The value of the net worth statement becomes clear when you examine the finances of Bob and Laura, a fictitious but very typical couple. They have been married for twenty years, have two children, and face some major questions in their financial life, such as how much to give, where to give, how to reduce taxes, how much life insurance to own, whether to participate in the company savings plan, how to reduce their debt, and what investments make sense for them now. To help begin the analysis, their assets and liabilities are listed and categorized as follows:

Assets: Bob & Laura

Chart 7-A

LIQUID ASSETS	
Cash on hand and checking account	$2,000
Money market funds	-0-
CDs	-0-
Savings (2% interest rate)	1,000
Marketable securities	-0-
Life insurance cash values	6,000
TOTAL LIQUID ASSETS	**$9,000**
NONLIQUID ASSETS	
Home (market value)	$112,000
Land (market value)	-0-
Business valuation	-0-
Real estate investments	15,000
Limited partnerships	-0-
Boat, camper, tractor, etc.	6,000
Automobile(s) (market value)	8,000
Furniture and personal property (estimated market value)	5,000
Coin & stamp collections, antiques	-0-
IRAs	-0-
Pension & profit sharing	-0-
Receivables from others	-0-
TOTAL NONLIQUID ASSETS	**$146,000**

Liabilities: Bob & Laura

Chart 7-B

CREDITOR	BALANCE DUE	INTEREST RATE	MONTHLY PAYMENT	LOAN DURATION
1. Credit cards	$3,000	18%	$50	Life
2. Auto loan	6,000	12%	263	3 Years
3. Parents	5,000	6%	—	?
4. Boat loan	5,000	14%	200	3 Years
5. Bank loan	13,500	15%	200	10 Years
6. Life insurance	5,000	5%	—	?
7. Home mortgage	81,000	9%	684	25 Years
8.				
9.				
TOTALS	$118,500		$1,397	

They listed their assets at a value they could be sold for and their liabilities at the current balance due. To come up with their net worth, Bob and Laura subtracted the total balance owed of $118,500 from the total of liquid and nonliquid assets of $155,000. They now have a net worth of $36,500. So what does this mean?

It means that they have some problems in their financial situation, which they may or may not have recognized. They have some strengths, which could be used to their advantage; they also need to take some action. (We analyzed their statement of net worth as follows.)

Net Worth Analysis: Bob & Laura

Chart 7-C

NET WORTH	$36,500
Liquid assets	$9,000
Nonliquid assets	146,000
TOTAL ASSETS	155,000
Less total liabilities	(118,500)
NET WORTH	$36,500
LIQUIDITY: For emergencies, bills, major purchases, and investment opportunities	$9,000

PRODUCTIVE ASSETS: Generating or having the potential to generate income	$24,000
Liquid assets	$9,000
Real estate	15,000
TOTAL PRODUCTIVE ASSETS	$24,000
PROPENSITY TO BORROW: Liabilities divided by assets $118,500 ÷ $155,000 =	76%

PROPENSITY TO ACCUMULATE: Net worth divided by years worked $36,500 ÷ 20yrs =	$1,825/year

Liquid Assets

When preparing the statement of net worth, one major category of assets is liquid assets—in other words, those assets that could be converted into cash immediately with no loss of principal. The person who has liquidity says, "I have financial flexibility in order to meet emergencies, unexpected bills, make major purchases, and take advantage of opportunities that come along." The more liquid the assets, the more flexible the person is—and probably more financially secure.

Our grandparents put most of their money in the bank because it was relatively safe and totally liquid. They had greater flexibility in their financial situation and greater security. However, there is a risk to having all of one's resources in the bank or invested in cash or cash-type investments. These risks will be covered in chapter 13, "Investment Planning."

Productive Assets

The next category of assets on the net worth statement includes those that are productive as opposed to those that are basically passive in nature. A productive asset generates or has the potential to generate income for investment purposes. Bob and Laura's listing of productive assets includes all of the liquid assets plus the real estate investment, for a total of $24,000. Some of their other assets may grow in value, such as their home, but that was not their primary reason for purchasing a home. The purpose of the home is to have a place to live, and it is typically not sold merely to produce income.

In comparing Bob and Laura's total productive assets of $24,000 to their total assets of $155,000, a rather typical picture emerges of a young couple who has invested, over time, their excess cash flow mostly in personal-type assets, as opposed to investment assets or productive assets. If Bob and Laura continue to follow the usual pattern as they grow older, the amount of their productive assets will grow in relation to their total assets because their family's needs are generally met sometime between the ages of thirty-five and fifty. After that point, the primary emphasis is on accumulating assets that can be used to fund retirement when it comes. Such assets are also more productive in nature than cars, boats, and homes.

Propensity to Borrow

Bob and Laura have a propensity to borrow—that is, their liabilities divided by their assets reveal they are 76 percent likely to borrow in order to add assets. In other words, 76 percent of their assets have been acquired by borrowing rather than by generating a positive cash-flow margin. (The lower the percentage of borrowing to acquire, the better the financial situation is. Zero percent means that there has been no borrowing to accumulate; 100 percent or greater means that there has been no excess cash flow and that all assets have been acquired by borrowing. It also means that this person or couple is bankrupt and could not meet their debts even if they sold everything.)

The propensity to borrow is a ratio that I have used in my financial analysis of other people's situations merely to point out that acquiring things is not the objective. That can be done through borrowed funds in many cases, but it does not mean that many things equal a secure financial situation. Debt against those things means that in reality they are not owned by the one who has them, but rather by the lender. As the biblical principle states: The borrower becomes the lender's slave.

Propensity to Accumulate

Another measurement I use in doing a financial analysis is the propensity to accumulate, which is calculated by dividing net worth by the number of years worked. It is merely an indicator of how much accumulation on the average has taken place each year. It also indicates where that couple might end up financially if they continued at that rate of accumulation.

For example, Bob and Laura's net worth of $36,500 divided by 20, the number of years that Bob has worked, means that they have been able to accumulate, on the average, $1,825 per year. If Bob still has thirty years of productivity left, and continues to accumulate at $1,825 per year, he will end up at retirement with a net worth of $54,750. However, if that amount of $1,825 can be compounded at a reasonable investment rate, they will have accumulated substantially more than $54,750. They are making progress toward the accomplishment of their long-term goals.

There is no right level for the propensity to accumulate because it depends upon the long-term goals, but the higher it is, the sooner you will achieve these long-term goals. Working through mathematically the propensity to borrow and the propensity to accumulate points out that the higher the debt ratio or propensity to borrow, the lower the propensity to accumulate. In other words, borrowing does not always help you to achieve your financial goals and objectives.

During the very first seminar on financial planning that I taught, an older couple was preparing their statement of net worth. I heard the wife say to the husband, "I didn't know we owned that," and a little bit later, "When did we buy that?" and somewhat later, "Why do we have that debt?" In talking with them later, I learned that the two of them had never prepared a statement of net worth together, and only the husband knew approximately where they stood financially. I have subsequently found that this is very common—that a husband and wife very rarely sit down and discuss where they are financially by looking at an actual statement of their net worth. I strongly urge every couple to annually prepare and review a statement of net worth.

Pointers in Preparing a Statement of Net Worth

You can use the forms on pages 87–88 of this book to complete and analyze your own statement of net worth. Some pointers in preparing such a statement are:

- ❖ Remember that a liquid asset is one that can be converted to cash immediately.
- ❖ Use estimates of the market value.
- ❖ Where market values are not known, use the original cost.
- ❖ Don't list the net values of investments and real estate owned since the liability will be listed under the liabilities section (list their market or paid value under assets).
- ❖ Consider stocks and bonds as marketable securities.
- ❖ List Individual Retirement Accounts (IRAs) and 401(k)s under nonliquid assets because there is a penalty for withdrawing these funds prematurely.
- ❖ Include pension and profit-sharing accounts that you have funded personally, or employer contributions in which you

are vested and are due you even if you left your current employer.

❖ In listing your debts, list long-term debts first—for example, the home mortgage.

❖ Don't include utility bills and monthly bills as a liability since these will be covered under the cash-flow summary. If you are behind on your utility payments or monthly bills, list the amount you are in arrears as a debt that is due.

Your Assets

Chart 7-D

LIQUID ASSETS	
Cash on hand and checking account	$
Money market funds	
CDs (interest rate ___%)	
Savings (____% interest rate)	
Marketable securities	
Life insurance cash values	
TOTAL LIQUID ASSETS	$
NONLIQUID ASSETS	
Home (market value)	$
Land (market value)	
Business valuation	
Real estate investments	
Limited partnerships	
Boat, camper, tractor, etc.	
Automobile(s) (market value)	
Furniture and personal property (estimated market value)	
Coin & stamp collections, antiques	
IRAs	
Pension & profit sharing	
Receivables from others	
TOTAL NONLIQUID ASSETS	$

Your Net Worth Analysis

Chart 7-E

NET WORTH	$
Liquid assets	
Nonliquid assets	
TOTAL ASSETS	
Less total liabilities	( )
NET WORTH	$
LIQUIDITY: For emergencies, bills, major purchases, and investment opportunities	$
PRODUCTIVE ASSETS: Generating or having the potential to generate income	$
Liquid assets	
Real estate	
TOTAL PRODUCTIVE ASSETS	$
PROPENSITY TO BORROW: Liabilities divided by assets	%
PROPENSITY TO ACCUMULATE: Net worth divided by years worked	$

Summary of Cash Flow

If the statement of net worth can be compared to a snapshot or an x-ray, then the summary of cash flow can be likened to a movie. Cash flow is not a measurement at a point in time like a net worth statement, but is rather a measurement of cash inflows and cash outflows over a defined period. Cash flow is either retrospective, a summary of what has happened over a period of time in the past, or it is prospective, a projection of what is going to happen over a period of time in the future.

Review again the Financial Planning Diagram on page 81 and notice that there are six elements to cash flow. First there is the inflow, which comes from salary, business income, earnings or investments, and pension retirement income; and then there are five outflows: giving, taxes, debt repayment, living expenses, and savings.

Cash Flow

We can examine the cash flow for Bob and Laura in five steps:

1. By projecting their income in Exhibit A;

2. By projecting their giving for the next twelve-month time period in Exhibit B;

3. By projecting their taxes for all types of taxes in Exhibit C;

4. By projecting their debt repayment in Exhibit D; and

5. By projecting their living expenses over the next twelve months in Exhibit E.

Exhibit A—Projected Income: Bob & Laura

Chart 7-F

GENERAL SOURCES	SPECIFIC SOURCES	MONTHLY INCOME	NON-MONTHLY INCOME	TOTAL ANNUAL INCOME
Gross wages	Husband	$3,750	$	$45,000
Gross wages	Wife		2,550	2,550
Dividends				
Dividends				
Dividends				
Interest	Savings		50	50
Interest				
Interest				
Rents				
Business				
Pensions/Annuities				
Other	Real Estate		2,000	2,000
Other				
Other				
TOTAL GROSS INCOME		$3,750	$4,600	$49,600

Exhibit B—Giving: Bob & Laura

Chart 7-G

GIVING CATEGORY	ORGANIZATION	MONTHLY GIVING	ANNUAL GIVING	TOTAL GIVING
Church		$50	$	$600
Other	Christian Org. (A)	20		240
Other	Christian Org. (B)		400	400
Other	Fishing Federation	80		960
Other				
Other				
Other				
Other				
Other				
Other				
Other				
Other				
TOTAL GIVING		$150	$400	$2,200

Exhibit C—Taxes: Bob & Laura   Chart 7-H

DEDUCTIONS, WITHHOLDINGS, AND ESTIMATES	MONTHLY WITHHOLDINGS	QUARTERLY ESTIMATES	TOTAL PAID
Federal income tax	$410	$0	$4,920
State and city income tax	138	0	1,656
Social Security and Medicare taxes	287	0	3,444
TOTAL TAX	$835	$0	$10,020

To review Bob and Laura's situation, their projected income (from Exhibit A) over the next twelve months is $3,750 per month from salaries and then $4,600, which is not received on a monthly basis, for a total annual amount of $49,600, which by itself looks pretty good. However, this is without considering the outflow.

You should also note that it was necessary to prepare the statement of net worth *first* in order not to miss the income from such things as interest on the savings account and the real estate investment, which generates a cash flow of $2,000 per year. In addition to salaries and wages, dividends, interest, etc., there may be sales of assets, pension plan liquidations, and commissions. Commissions are difficult to project because they are unknown. My recommendation is that couples project commission income on a conservative basis as they estimate a projected cash flow.

Giving

The giving amounts from Exhibit B are again of two types: those that are given on a normal monthly basis, and those that are given on some other basis, such as annually, as a result of an appeal or pledge that has been made previously. The total indicates that Bob and Laura are projecting to give $2,200 for the next year.

Taxes

The tax summary that is projected for Bob and Laura includes all income taxes and Social Security taxes, but not property taxes or other types of taxes. The information with which to prepare this summary came from their pay stubs. (In addition to tax withholdings, a person might be subject to tax estimates, which are paid on a quarterly basis.) In the case of Bob and Laura, they are paying a total of $835 per month of tax withholdings or $10,020 on an annual basis.

Exhibit D—Debt Repayment: Bob & Laura   Chart 7-I

CREDITOR	BALANCE DUE	INTEREST RATE	MONTHLY PAYMENT	LOAN DURATION
1. Credit cards	$3,000	18%	$50	Life
2. Auto loan	6,000	12%	263	3 Years
3. Parents	5,000	6%	–	?
4. Boat loan	5,000	14%	200	3 Years
5. Bank loan	13,500	15%	200	10 Years
6. Life insurance	5,000	5%	–	?
7.				
8.				
9.				
TOTALS	$37,500		$713	

Exhibit E—Living Expenses: Bob & Laura   Chart 7-J

	MONTHLY PAYMENTS	NON-MONTHLY PAYMENTS	TOTAL ANNUAL AMOUNT
HOUSING			
Mortgage/rent	$684	$	$8,208
Insurance	–	400	400
Property taxes	–	1,000	1,000
Electricity	60		720
Heating	40		480
Water	30		360
Sanitation	–		–
Telephone	40		480
Cleaning	–		–
Repairs/maintenance	20		240
Supplies	10		120
Improvements	–		–
Furnishings	50		600
Total Housing	$934	$1,400	$12,608
FOOD Total Food	$400	$	$4,800
CLOTHING Total Clothing	$	$1,000	$1,000
TRANSPORTATION			
Insurance	$	$500	$500
Gas and oil	150		1,800
Maintenance/repairs	30		360
Parking			
Other			
Total Transportation	$180	$500	$2,660

	MONTHLY PAYMENTS	NON-MONTHLY PAYMENTS	TOTAL ANNUAL AMOUNT
ENTERTAINMENT / RECREATION			
Eating out	$40	$	$480
Babysitters	10		120
Magazines/newspapers	20		240
Vacation		1,000	1,000
Clubs and activities		300	300
Total Entertainment/Rec.	$70	$1,300	$2,140
MEDICAL EXPENSES			
Insurance	$60	$	$720
Doctors	20		240
Dentists	20		240
Drugs	5		60
Other			
Total Medical	$105	$	$1,260
INSURANCE			
Life	$128	$	$1,536
Disability			
Total Insurance	$128	$	$1,536
CHILDREN			
School lunches	$30	$	$360
Allowances	20		240
Tuition and college		6,000	6,000
Lessons	20		240
Other	5		60
Other	5		60
Total Children	$80	$6,000	$6,960
GIFTS			
Christmas	$	$500	$500
Birthdays		150	150
Anniversary		200	200
Other	25		300
Total Gifts	$25	$850	$1,150
MISCELLANEOUS			
Toiletries	$25	$	$300
Husband: lunches & misc.	20		240
Wife: miscellaneous	20		240
Dry cleaning	20		240
Animals (license, food, vet)	10		120
Beauty and barber	20		240
Other			

	MONTHLY PAYMENTS	NON-MONTHLY PAYMENTS	TOTAL ANNUAL AMOUNT
Other			
Total Miscellaneous	$115	$	$1,380

TOTAL LIVING EXPENSES	$2,037	$11,050	$35,494

Debt Repayment

Exhibit D, the debt repayment schedule, is the same schedule as prepared for the liability section of the net worth statement, with the exception that the mortgage loan amount has been left out and is not included in the total. The mortgage loan payment is included in the living expenses section in Exhibit E. In some cases no payment is being made or is intended to be made, and therefore it is not included in the payment schedule. For example, the loan from the parents—there is no intention on Bob and Laura's part of repaying that loan. (Parents beware!) Additionally, the life insurance loan will not be repaid; therefore it shows no payment. Bob and Laura are paying $713 per month in debt repayment, which includes principal and interest and does not include the home mortgage. The annual debt repayment amount, then, is $8,556, more if Bob and Laura include their debt to parents, which they should rightly do—if not now, as soon as possible.

Cash Flow Analysis: Bob & Laura

Chart 7-K

GROSS INCOME: From Exhibit A (page 89)	$49,600

LESS EXPENSES	$(20,776)
Giving—from Exhibit B (page 89)	(2,200)
Taxes—from Exhibit C (page 90)	(10,020)
Debt—from Exhibit D (page 91)	(8,556)
TOTAL EXPENSES	(20,776)
NET SPENDABLE INCOME	$28,824
LESS LIVING EXPENSES: From Exhibit E (pages 91 to 93)	$(35,494)
Housing	(12,608)
Food	(4,800)
Clothing	(1,000)
Transportation	(2,660)
Entertainment & recreation	(2,140)

Medical	(1,260)
Insurance	(1,536)
Children	(6,960)
Gifts	(1,150)
Miscellaneous	(1,380)
TOTAL LIVING EXPENSES	(35,494)
CASH-FLOW MARGIN	$(6,670)

Living Expenses

Exhibit E, the living expense schedule for Bob and Laura, shows monthly living expenses of $2,037 for the twelve-month period. Expenses paid other than monthly are $11,050, for a total annual living expense of $35,494.

Their mortgage payment is included under housing expenses, while the car payment is not included under transportation because it is included under the debt repayment schedule, Exhibit D. (Car payments are generally considered a more discretionary type of expense.) In every case, Bob and Laura estimated their expenses, and for the monthly amounts, they estimated average expenses.

Cash-Flow Margin

Bob and Laura can now summarize each of the exhibits into a cash flow analysis as illustrated on pages 93–94. Two primary observations emerge from this summary. First of all, the cash-flow margin after all living expenses are subtracted from the gross income is a negative $6,670. This means that with no further planning on their part, they will have to do one of four things: (1) increase their income, (2) reduce their expenses, (3) dip into their savings, or (4) borrow additional monies in order not to have a negative cash flow for the year (but this only compounds the problem).

Since Bob and Laura are typical, the chances are pretty good that they did not even know they were running a cash-flow margin that was negative. It probably crept up on them month by month. They also probably increased their credit card debt. They may even be considering using a debt consolidation loan, or Laura may look for work outside the home, or they may reduce their giving. Now that the problem has been defined, the solution is much easier to determine.

Net Spendable Income

In addition to the cash-flow margin, this summary uses the concept of Net Spendable Income. The net spendable income basically says that the first three priority uses of money are giving, taxes, and debt repayment. The amount of spendable income, then, is the amount left. The net spendable income concept establishes the priorities of income and says that living expenses should be the fourth priority, as opposed to typically being the first.

Giving should be proportionate and should come out of the first fruits (see 1 Corinthians 16:2; Proverbs 3:9). Taxes are an obligation to the believer and therefore a priority (see Romans 13:7). Debt repayment is a must for the believer (see Psalm 37:21). If Scripture gives us these three priorities, then living expenses are discretionary, manageable, and thus, a fourth priority.

Where Are You?

Remember that we are not yet ready to work on solutions. We are still in the process of determining where you are. Using the charts on pages 97 through 101 you can prepare your own cash-flow summary. Some guidelines are as follows:

Exhibit A: Your Projected Income

1. The amounts should be derived from gross income before taxes and other deductions.

2. To determine monthly amounts:

   a. If you are paid on a weekly basis, use one week's pay multiplied by 4.3 (weeks per month).

   b. If you are paid every two weeks, you get twenty-six paychecks per year. Multiply your two-week paycheck by 2.17. This will compensate for the two months of the year in which you receive three paychecks.

   c. If the checks received are not always the same, owing to irregular hours (overtime, shift differential, etc.), use an average pay per month as the salary.

   d. If your pay is on a commission-only basis, use an average of the past few years or what you consider a reasonable (not hopeful) income projection.

3. Dividends and interest income should be projected as annual amounts unless these funds are being received on a monthly basis.

4. Rents received should be shown as "net rents"—in other words, rental income less all rental payments and expenses.

5. Include other income from all sources, such as babysitting, hobbies, crafts, and gifts.

6. Business income may consist of income from self-employment, income-producing hobbies, or other business interests.

Exhibit B: Your Giving

1. Project your giving for the year by considering each organization you support. Use the amount of pledges, a percentage of income, past giving history, or specific giving goals in your projection.

Exhibit C: Taxes

1. The best source for determining taxes is pay stubs. Use the withholdings per check and multiply by the number of pay periods per year as described for Exhibit A.

2. Tax refunds received from overpayments in the previous year should be shown as an income source. If this is regularly happening, for the next year, increase your deductions to have less taxes paid and more to use for other needs. More on taxes in chapter 12.

3. If you are self-employed or have self-employment income, estimate your annual taxes.

4. Self-employment and Social Security taxes can be determined from the following chart:

2004 Social Security and Medicare Taxes   Chart 7-L

EARNINGS SUBJECT TO TAX		PAYMENT BY EMPLOYER AND EMPLOYEE		PAID BY SELF-EMPLOYED PERSON	
	WAGE BASE	RATE	MAXIMUM TAX	RATE	MAXIMUM TAX
SS Tax	$0–$87,900	6.20%	$5,050	12.40%	$10,900
Medicare	Unlimited	1.45%	Unlimited	2.90%	Unlimited

Exhibit D: Debt Payment

1. Do not forget to adjust for any debts that will be completely paid during the year.

Exhibit E: Living Expenses

1. Many expenses, such as utilities, should be monthly averages.

2. Use estimates if you are unsure exactly what is being spent. The objective is to aim for 80 percent accuracy on your initial try.

3. Note that transportation expense does not include debt repayment because the auto payments are accounted for under Exhibit D.

Cash-Flow Margin:

1. Note the section for listing existing cash-flow margin commitments. This might include payroll deductions, such as retirement programs, pretax medical plans, stock purchase plans, or other investments that require regular payments.

2. Funds allocated to credit unions, payroll savings plans, or deposited to savings accounts are uncommitted funds since they have no specific purpose and are available for reallocation.

Your Cash Flow Analysis: Year_____   Chart 7-M

GROSS INCOME: From Exhibit A (page 98)	$
LESS EXPENSES	$( )
Giving—from Exhibit B (page 99)	
Taxes—from Exhibit C (page 99)	
Debt—from Exhibit D (page 99)	
TOTAL EXPENSES	
NET SPENDABLE INCOME	$
LESS LIVING EXPENSES: From Exhibit E (pages 100 to 101)	$( )
Housing	( )
Food	( )
Clothing	( )
Transportation	( )
Entertainment/Recreation	( )

Medical	(	)
Insurance	(	)
Children	(	)
Gifts	(	)
Miscellaneous	(	)
TOTAL LIVING EXPENSES		
CASH-FLOW MARGIN: Net spendable less living expenses	$	

EXISTING MARGIN COMMITMENTS	$
Company savings plan	
IRA	
Investment commitments	
TOTAL EXISTING MARGIN COMMITMENTS	
UNCOMMITTED MARGIN	$

Exhibit A—Your Projected Income

Chart 7-N

GENERAL SOURCES	SPECIFIC SOURCES	MONTHLY INCOME	NON-MONTHLY INCOME	TOTAL ANNUAL INCOME
Gross wages	Husband			
Gross wages	Wife			
Dividends				
Dividends				
Dividends				
Interest				
Interest				
Interest				
Rents				
Business				
Pensions/annuities				
Other				
Other				
TOTAL GROSS INCOME				

Exhibit B—Your Giving

Chart 7-O

GIVING CATEGORY	ORGANIZATION	MONTHLY GIVING	ANNUAL GIVING	TOTAL GIVING
Church				
Other				
Other				
Other				
Other				
Other				
Other				
Other				
Other				
Other				
Other				
Other				
	TOTAL GIVING			

Exhibit C—Your Taxes

Chart 7-P

DEDUCTIONS, WITHHOLDINGS, AND ESTIMATES	MONTHLY WITHHOLDINGS	QUARTERLY ESTIMATES	TOTAL PAID
Federal income tax			
State and city income tax			
Social Security and Medicare taxes			
TOTAL TAX			

Exhibit D—Debt Payment

Chart 7-Q

CREDITOR	BALANCE DUE	INTEREST RATE	MONTHLY PAYMENT	LOAN DURATION
1.				
2.				
3.				
4.				
5.				
6.				
7.				
8.				
9.				
TOTALS				

Exhibit E—Living Expenses: Year:_____   Chart 7-R

	MONTHLY PAYMENTS	NON-MONTHLY PAYMENTS	TOTAL ANNUAL AMOUNT
HOUSING			
Mortgage/rent			
Insurance			
Property taxes			
Electricity			
Heating			
Water			
Sanitation			
Telephone			
Cleaning			
Repairs/maintenance			
Supplies			
Improvements			
Furnishings			
Total Housing*			
FOOD			
CLOTHING			
TRANSPORTATION			
Insurance			
Gas and oil			
Maintenance/repairs			
Parking			
Other			
Total Transportation*			
ENTERTAINMENT/RECREATION			
Eating out			
Babysitters			
Magazines/newspapers			
Vacation			
Clubs and activities			
Total Entertainment/Rec.*			
MEDICAL EXPENSES			
Insurance			
Doctors			
Dentists			
Drugs			
Other			
Total Medical*			

Permission is granted to photocopy this page.

	MONTHLY PAYMENTS	NON-MONTHLY PAYMENTS	TOTAL ANNUAL AMOUNT
INSURANCE			
Life			
Disability			
Total Insurance*			
CHILDREN			
School lunches			
Allowances			
Tuition and college			
Lessons			
Other			
Other			
Total Children*			
GIFTS			
Christmas			
Birthdays			
Anniversary			
Other			
Total Gifts*			
MISCELLANEOUS			
Toiletries			
Husband: lunches & misc.			
Wife: miscellaneous			
Dry cleaning			
Animals (license, food, vet)			
Beauty and barber			
Other			
Other			
Total Miscellaneous*			
TOTAL LIVING EXPENSES			

*Transfer the totals to the cash flow analysis chart on pages 97–98

Life Insurance Summary

So far we have summarized Bob and Laura's financial situation and you have completed your own cash-flow analysis. You assume you are going to continue to live. However, there are two other alternatives—one is death and the other is what has been called "living death" or disability. Disability insurance is insuring your paycheck. If you were injured in a car wreck and were unable to work for a few

Life Insurance: Bob & Laura

Chart 7-S

COMPANY	ISSUE DATE	POLICY #	TYPE (1)	INSURED	OWNER	BENEFI-CIARY	WAIVER OF PREMIUM	FACE VALUE	CASH VALUE	CASH VALUE BORROWED	YEARLY PREMIUMS
Personal											
So. Trust	8/2/64	12345	Whole	H	H	W	Yes	2,000	1,000	-0-	36
Eternal Life	8/10/86	53210	Whole	H	H	W	Yes	25,000	2,500	2,500	400
Family Life	8/22/92	97531	Whole	H	H	W	Yes	50,000	2,500	2,500	900
Family Life	8/22/92	97532	Term	W	W	H	Yes	50,000	—	—	200
Retirement Plan											
Business											
Work Co.	10/20/88	?	Group Term	H	Comp.	W	Yes	10,000			
Mortgage											

(1) Term, whole life, endowment, group, etc.
Do you apply dividends to reduce premium payment?
Are there any special features on any of the policies? (Is it paid up? guaranteed insurability rider, etc.?)

years, disability insurance benefits would pay you a percentage—usually 60-80 percent—of your salary. You may buy an individual disability insurance policy or buy group long-term disability insurance through your employer.

In chapter 14 we will look more closely at making decisions about life insurance protection and in determining how much is needed, why it is needed, and what kind to buy. But at this point let's see where Bob and Laura stand in the summary of their life insurance on page 102.

Sources and Types of Life Insurance

There are four sources of life insurance that Bob and Laura could have: policies that are owned personally, policies that are part of a retirement plan, policies owned by the company for which Bob works, and mortgage life insurance on the home mortgage. There are also various basic types of life insurance that could be owned; whole life, endowment, term, group term, and universal life are some.

Face Value and Cash Value

Face value is usually the death benefit. Cash value is the surrender value of the policy if it were to be cashed in; and cash value borrowed is the amount of money that has been borrowed on that cash value. The cash value borrowed reduces the death benefit by the amount borrowed plus interest.

The blank form on page 104 will allow you to complete your own insurance summary and analysis.

Conclusion

Step 1 of the financial planning process has been completed. You have determined where you are by summarizing your present situation. But you don't stay where you are—you move forward. You may have heard it said that a form of mental illness is doing the same thing over and over again and expecting a different result. By this analysis we have identified your obvious problems, financial strengths, and some action steps. Before determining what action steps to take and which problems to focus on, you need to know what your goals and priorities are. That's the best way to head down the right path.

Your Life Insurance

Chart 7-T

COMPANY	ISSUE DATE	POLICY #	TYPE (1)	INSURED	OWNER	BENEFI-CIARY	WAIVER OF PREMIUM	FACE VALUE	CASH VALUE	CASH VALUE BORROWED	YEARLY PREMIUMS
Personal											
Retirement Plan											
Business											
Mortgage											

(1) Term, whole life, endowment, group, etc.
Do you apply dividends to reduce premium payment? _____
Are there any special features on any of the policies? (Is it paid up? guaranteed insurability rider, etc.?)

8

SETTING FAITH FINANCIAL GOALS

"Aim at nothing and you will hit it every time."
ANONYMOUS

"Our goals can only be reached through a vehicle of a plan, in which we must fervently believe, and upon which we must vigorously act. There is no other route to success."
PABLO PICASSO

"When it is obvious that the goals cannot be reached, don't adjust the goals, adjust the action steps."
CONFUCIUS

John Goddard is an interesting man who "wanted to do it all." As a fifteen-year-old in Los Angeles, he drew up a list of everything he wanted to accomplish in his life. He had a vision of himself as a great explorer and put down such things as: explore the Nile, climb Mount Everest, retrace the travels of Marco Polo and Alexander the Great, visit every country in the world, visit the moon. His list had a total of 127 goals.

Now nearly seventy-five, Goddard still lives in southern California, but he has made many expeditions and is an author and lecturer. He smiles when asked about the list he made years ago.

"Nearly everyone," he says, "has goals and dreams, but not everyone acts on them. There are things on it I will never do, like climb Mount Everest or star in a Tarzan movie. Goal setting is like that. Some may be beyond your capabilities, but that doesn't mean you have to give up the whole dream."

Although Goddard believes in accomplishment, he does not feel compelled to complete every item on his list. He suggests that goals be guidelines, but not something to control one's life. Goddard also thinks that it is helpful to look at your life and ask, "If I had one more year to live, what would I do?" To date, Goddard has completed 109 of his 127 goals. Has he failed because he has not finished his list? To the contrary, his list has inspired his many successes.

We all set goals and objectives—at least informally—and develop plans to achieve them. None of us ever start a vacation without knowing where we want to go, or plant a garden without knowing what we want to come up. We wouldn't just scatter seeds around, hoping something will come up, or build a home without giving the architect and builder any instructions—just leaving them to their own judgment. Almost anyone would say that goals are important, and yet studies have shown that less than 3 percent of Americans have written goals.

I believe there are four vital reasons goals should be set and also four reasons we don't set them. This chapter will take us from the reasons for setting goals, to the barriers to setting them, and then to the practical application of setting a faith goal.

Four Vital Reasons for Goals

The first and most obvious reason for setting goals is that goals provide direction and purpose. They are finish lines. Have you ever seen a sprinter start down the track and stop and look for the finish line? Of course not! Sprinters know exactly where they are headed, and all of their efforts are directed toward the accomplishment of the goal. When we set goals, our choices for activity become purposeful with more potential of being God-directed. Otherwise, circumstances, other people, and feelings determine where we wind up.

Second, goals help us to crystallize our thinking. Judy and I often challenge each other with the statement, "If you aim at nothing, you will hit it every time." When you set a goal, you tend to crystallize your thinking about what you really want to accomplish. This is why I believe that goals should be written, rather than merely thought or talked about.

Third, goals provide personal motivation. When I went to Indiana University in 1960, I had an objective: to have a good time. I accomplished that objective, but in the process I was asked a couple of times to leave school. My grade point average hovered around the failing level. When I came back to school, met my future wife, and began to think about marriage, I also began to think about career objectives. I set a goal to become a Certified Public Accountant (CPA). My grade point average went from failing to almost straight A's, and I ultimately graduated from graduate school with honors.

After college, when I was interviewing for jobs, the interviewers often asked me what happened. The only thing I could tell them was that I finally had a goal. I had not changed personally, but the goal toward which I was moving had changed and so provided motivation in a better direction.

A goal is a statement of God's will for me. This is the fourth reason to set goals. Goals are all stated as future objectives, and only God lives in the future. So when I set a goal, I have implicitly made a statement that says, "God willing, I believe I should achieve the following . . ." Otherwise, for a Christian, a goal is presumption.

Paul was probably one of the most goal-oriented men in the Bible. He said in Philippians 3:14: "I press toward the goal for the prize of the upward call of God in Christ Jesus." Paul knew why he was there and where he was going; his life was governed by his goal.

Almost anyone would say that goals are important. Why, then, don't we set goals?

Four Barriers to Goal Setting

Many of us don't set goals because we fear failure. If a goal is not set, there is no chance of failing to meet it. This is no excuse for anyone to not set goals—especially for a Christian. In the mere act of becoming a Christian, one has admitted the inability to govern his or her life. However, the fear of failure is so dominant a part of our fallen nature that it, maybe more than any other motivation, governs our behavior and is a principal reason goals are not set.

The second reason we don't set goals is the false assumption that goal setting must take a great deal of time. A little book entitled *Tyranny of the Urgent* by Charles E. Hummel has as its thesis that we get involved in urgent but trivial matters and leave the really important things undone. We often treat goal setting like that. Even if it took a substantial amount of time, it would be worth setting aside the time.

As a matter of fact, we spend much of our lives thinking about goals and objectives, but because we never write them down, we never move toward accomplishing them. The actual process of writing down goals takes only a few minutes. We are merely getting them out of our heads and onto paper.

The third reason that goals are not set is a legitimate one—we don't know what goals to set. This is especially true in the financial area because so much advice is being given, both good and bad, that we become confused. As Christians we can determine which goals to set, we can set them, and then we can develop a plan of action to achieve them. We have already looked at the Financial Planning Diagram (see page 120) and examined the eleven goals areas—five short-term and six long-term goals.

I used to play golf in a very competitive environment with my partners and staff members in the CPA firm. On one occasion we were playing to a hole with an elevated green. We could actually "see" the hole from the fairway only by seeing the top of the flagstick indicating where the hole was. As our foursome finished the hole, one of us took the flagstick and stuck it in the soft ground on the edge of the green near a sand trap. Well, you can imagine what happened. The following foursome, not being able to see the hole, all placed their shots to the flagstick, and ended up in the sand trap.

Like that foursome, you may have a good game plan for achieving a goal and take the right steps to achieve it, but if the goal is a wrong one, then the results can be disastrous. It is *vitally important* to know what goals to set; otherwise, activity and decisions will be channeled toward the wrong objectives.

Finally, we do not set goals because many of us do not know how to set goals. We do not have a goal-setting process, and that also is a legitimate reason for not setting a goal.

What Not to Do

When we learn the process of how to set goals from a faith perspective, we need to look at three things *not to do*. Isaiah 43:18 says, "Forget the former things; do not dwell on the past." In setting a goal, first of all, we do not focus on the past. Focusing on the past tends to limit our thinking and emotions to our past experiences and our past failures. More importantly, focusing on the past leaves God out of the process. It is like saying, "Since I didn't do what He wanted in the past, then my future is forever marked by past failure." We're all tempted with such self-defeating thoughts, but we need to recognize that they are not God's truth about His grace or His plan for our future. Yes, we may deal with consequences from our past, but not with condemnation and guaranteed rejection or defeat because of it. "Now to him who is able to do immeasurably more than all we ask or imagine, according to his power that is at work within us" (Ephesians 3:20 NIV). God is never limited by what has gone on in the past. He wants to do something beyond what we can even think or imagine.

In Luke 1:18 we read the question of Zechariah to the angel in the temple: "How can I be sure of this? I am an old man and my wife is well along in years." Zechariah was focusing on his present resources, and that is the second thing we do *not* want to do in setting a goal. Focusing on our present resources is another way we limit God. The real question is, what are God's resources? Recall again Ephesians 3:20: "Now to him who is able to do immeasurably more than all we ask or imagine, according to his power that is at work within us." My present resources do not limit what He can do. He has limitless resources.

The last thing not to do in setting goals relates to those who are married. I believe that a couple should never set a goal apart from or in disagreement with one another. Most women will become widows, and if a woman has not been involved in the goal-setting process, the consequences can be devastating for both the woman and for the family. God puts a man and woman together to build something new, not to put two competing individuals together so that one can force goals and objectives upon the other—or keep the other in the dark to assert independence. In the marriage relationship a couple can set goals that are unique to the couple, not to one of the individuals in the marriage. "Live in harmony with one another" (Romans 12:16 NIV). The reality is that committing goals to paper in a marriage relationship requires unity and agreement, which are threatening to many people.

Setting Your Faith Goals

I define a faith goal as "an objective toward which I believe God wants me to move." It is asking, "God, what are your plans?" or saying, "God, I am available—not necessarily able, but available." Setting faith goals is a three-step process.

1. Spend Time with God

One of our critical needs in the Christian life is to spend time with our Lord in communion with Him, seeking His will and direction. God's Word clearly says that if we seek His will and direction, He will respond by giving us that direction.

> Do not conform any longer to the pattern of this world, but be transformed by the renewing of your mind. Then you will be able to test and approve what God's will is—his good, pleasing and perfect will. —Romans 12:2 NIV

> Ask, and it will be given to you; seek, and you will find; knock, and the door will be opened to you. For everyone who asks receives, and he who seeks finds, and to him who knocks, the door will be opened. —Matthew 7:7–8 NIV

> Come near to God and He will come near to you. —James 4:8 NIV

Spending time with God is essential; otherwise, goal setting without God's direction becomes merely striving after your own imagination and dreams. A faith goal is a statement of *God's will* as far as we understand and perceive it.

2. Record the Impressions

As you spend time with God, you need to record what He seems to be saying to you. You need to take this second step, because over time, as you record the impressions you receive, assurance and conviction will result. "Now faith is being sure of what we hope for and certain of what we do not see" (Hebrews 11:1 NIV). You need to be continually asking God, "What would You have me do?" but not, "How would You have me do it?" As you record the answers He gives you, you become more and more certain of the goal. It is essential to have the goal recorded, because very likely there will be testing. God's objective is to build your faith, and testing does it!

3. Make the Goal Measurable

After spending time with God and recording what He seems to be saying to you, you are ready to set a faith goal. The objective toward which you believe God wants you to move must be *measurable*. For example, to be a good father is not a goal but a purpose statement. To spend fifteen minutes a day with each of my children is a goal. That can be measured. Because goals are measurable, we know definitely when they have been achieved. If you cannot determine when a goal has been achieved, then it was not a goal—it was an intention or a purpose statement.

There are several reasons to make goals measurable. First of all, a measurable goal gives a standard of accountability. If the goal is not measurable, there is no way you can be accountable for achieving it, and it becomes meaningless. Second, in a marriage relationship, a measurable goal can only be achieved by mutual agreement. Yet one of the major problems I experience in financial counseling with couples is what I call "goal incongruity," which relates to this very issue and is, in most cases, unintentional. Goal incongruity occurs when a husband and wife have goals that are not identical. Therefore, at best, they are working to accomplish inconsistent goals and, at worst, conflicting goals.

Once you have spent time with God, recorded what He seems to be saying to you, and set a measurable objective, you have a faith goal—"an objective toward which I believe God wants me to move."

4. Take Action

Faith, in itself, is *acting* on the basis of what God wants you to do. *Faith* is an action word.

A faith goal will typically have three characteristics. The first characteristic is that *its means of accomplishment* may not be evident. You may not be able to see how it will happen. "By faith Noah, when warned about things not yet seen, in holy fear built an ark to save his family" (Hebrews 11:7 NIV). Noah had never seen rain and certainly did not know how God was going to send a universal flood, but in response to God's initiative, Noah prepared an ark. He had faith that God was going to do what He said He was going to do.

Second, in many cases a faith goal may be set with inadequate resources. A story similar to that of Zechariah in the temple is found in Hebrews 11:11: "By faith Abraham, even though he was past age— and Sarah herself was barren—was enabled to become a father because he considered him faithful who had made the promise." Setting a faith goal may mean there are "apparently" no adequate resources to accomplish that goal. If it is God's goal, it is God's responsibility to provide the resources.

Of course, you do not test God by dreaming up goals or making foolish financial commitments that are inconsistent with Scripture; that is why the *process* of setting the goal is so important. When you spend time with Him, you receive assurance and conviction that this is what He would have you do. Therefore, resources are of no concern. They are God's responsibility. You do not set the goal and then go to Him asking for the resources. You let Him speak to you and develop the goal, and then you trust Him for the resources.

A faith goal will typically require setting an objective without fully understanding it. "By faith Abraham, when called to go to a place he would later receive as his inheritance, obeyed and went, even though he did not know where he was going" (Hebrews 11:8 NIV). Abraham did not know where he was going, but he went in response to God's initiative. The goals that you set by faith in the financial area of your life may also need to be set without full understanding about how they will be achieved with present resources. But many of the heroes of faith in Hebrews 11 experienced the same uncertainty.

What is required on your part are two things: First, trust that God will do His part, and second, take action by making a first step. Abraham, Noah, Sarah, Nehemiah, Daniel, David—all exercised faith by taking a first step of action in complete dependence upon God and without full understanding, adequate resources, or seeing how their goal could be accomplished. What was required was merely the first step. God then showed the second step, and then He showed the third step.

Again, the order of the *process* is essential:

❖ Spend time with God.

❖ Record what He is saying to you.

❖ Set a measurable goal.

❖ Take the first action step.

The results of following this process are that the goal will be reached, growth will be experienced, and God will be glorified.

Why? Because, first, it is God's goal, and second, He is committed to your growth as a Christian. Third, He will share His glory with no one, and it is *His* goal, and therefore He should receive the glory. *This means that God may not do it in the way that you think He should do it, or in the way that you would do it.* Give God the flexibility to do things His way, with His timing and His resources.

Vision for the Future: Bob & Laura

Chart 8-A

In five years, we see the following taking place:

GIVING
☒ We would be giving 10% per year.
☐ We would be making additional gifts each year of:	
☒ We would have made total gifts of:	$2,000 for the new chapel

COLLEGE			
☒ A college fund would exist for each of our children:			
Child	Type of College	Approximate Annual Cost	Total Cost
Sue	State college	$6,000	$24,000

LIFESTYLE DESIRES	
☒ We would have made the following major purchases: (new home, car, vacations, etc.)	
Item	Amount
Replace Laura's car	$5,000
Redecorate living room	$5,000
Buy a new house	$20,000

☒ We would have the following type of lifestyle: (increase, decrease, or maintain present level)

Maintain our present lifestyle.

PAY OFF DEBT	
☒ We would have paid off the following debts:	
Owed to	Total
Credit cards	$3,000
Boat loan	5,000
Bank loan	13,500
Parents' loan	5,000
Auto loan	6,000
Life insurance	5,000

BEGIN BUSINESS		
☐ We will have started our own business, which will require an investment of:		

FINANCIAL INDEPENDENCE		
☒ We will have the following investments:		
Type of Investment	Amount Invested	Annual Return
Emergency fund	$5,000	$5,000
☒ I would like to pass on to my spouse (children) the following estate:		
$100,000		
☐ We will have the adequate investment income to support our lifestyle of:	$	per month

When I was initially developing my own understanding of the concept and philosophy of biblical financial planning, I shared with my family this goal-setting process. At that time, our church was having a missions conference and our second daughter, Denise, wanted to make a pledge to the missions committee. She assured Judy and me that she had gone through the process of spending time with God, recording what He had said, and felt that He would have her pledge $2 a week. As Judy and I discussed it, we realized a problem existed—our daughter only received an allowance of $1 a week. Judy and I spent an afternoon trying to determine how we were going to "help God out" and to keep Him from being embarrassed, because, obviously, Denise could not fulfill that pledge. Of course, after a while, we realized what we were doing and stepped back to see what God would do.

Six months passed, and I had forgotten about the pledge. One day Judy asked me if I realized that Denise had made her pledge of $2 every week. By the end of the year, she had literally given $104. I know that money did not come out of her savings account, because I had control of that account. Frankly, I don't know where the money came from—and it is not important. The point is that she did what she believed God would have her do—one step at a time. She did not have to see how it was going to be accomplished, and she did not have to have the resources, nor did she have to understand the process of financial planning in order to get it accomplished. At the end of the year, the pledge was fulfilled, her spiritual growth was hastened, and God received all the glory.

As adults, we face the temptation of thinking the goal is insurmountable, and we forget who it came from. My primary recommendation when setting a goal is to never set the goal "in concrete"; rather "write it in sand on the seashore," because life is a process and God is dealing with us during this process. He can give us directions more easily if we move than if we sit still, waiting for Him to write a letter of instructions (which, in fact, He already has!).

To determine specifically where we are going financially, look again at the Financial Planning Diagram on page 120. In the long term, there are only six goals that can be set:

1. giving,

2. providing a college education for your children,

3. paying off debt,

4. accomplishing lifestyle desires,

5. beginning your own business, and

6. achieving financial independence.

Each of these goals, because of its financial nature, can be expressed in specific terms, and can therefore meet the criterion of being measurable.

With these six goals in mind, I have designed a Vision for the Future chart with space to answer questions under each goal-setting area. Each statement is preceded with: "In five years we see the following taking place." The chart is shown on pages 113 and 114 with answers from Bob and Laura as an illustration.

Use this chart to aid you in your goal-setting process. Remember that goal setting is a prayerful process, and it is a time for discussion between husband and wife to ensure congruity of goals. One way to start is for each of you, independently, to consider the goals and then discuss them together to develop a final version with joint agreement on the priorities of the goals.

My Vision for the Future

Chart 8-B

By_____(date), I see the following taking place:

GIVING
We would be giving __% per year.
We would be making additional gifts each year of:
We would have made total gifts of:

COLLEGE
A college fund would exist for each of our children:

Child	Type of College	Approximate Annual Cost	Total Cost

LIFESTYLE DESIRES
We would have made the following major purchases: (new home, car, vacations, etc.)

Item	Amount

We would have the following type of lifestyle: (increase, decrease, or maintain present level)

PAY OFF DEBT
We would have paid off the following debts:

Owed to	Total

BEGIN BUSINESS
We will have started our own business, which will require an investment of:

FINANCIAL INDEPENDENCE
We will have the following investments:

Type of Investment	Amount Invested	Annual Return

I would like to pass on to my spouse (children) the following estate:	
$	
We will have the adequate investment income to support our lifestyle of:	$ per month

If you do not have specific goals in mind, put down what comes to your mind first as you consider each of the areas shown on the chart. As you pray about these goals, God may lead you to change some or eliminate some. Be flexible and remember that this is the beginning of a process that will continue as long as you live. It cannot be completed at a point in time. Ultimately, God will reveal to you His priorities regarding your financial goals, and these priorities will be different for each individual and couple. Our financial goals are as unique as we are.

Your goal may be debt repayment, increasing giving, saving to give a significant gift, or renovating your home. Remember, no goal is more "spiritual" than another. If you are giving Him your hopes and asking Him to mold your dreams and you sense His permission and leading to do something more family- or home-centered—don't immediately discard those thoughts as self-centered. God delights in seeing you delight in watching Him move on your behalf. That renovated kitchen may be a wide open door of testimony and encouragement that He purposes for you and that He will provide for in time. Write it out, commit it to Him, and wait. I promise that ride will be more thrilling than the heavy noose of consumer debt on a remodeling loan.

Conclusion

At this point you know where you are and you know what God would have you do financially. The next step is to begin the action steps to accomplish the goals that God has given you. Remember, you don't have to see *how*. You may not have the resources, yet you can take action without full understanding, knowing that God is in control.

❖ You will reach the goal.

❖ You will experience spiritual growth.

❖ You will glorify God.

AVOIDING THE MOST COMMON FINANCIAL MISTAKES

"Often all it takes to start down the road to bankruptcy is a small raise in pay."
ANONYMOUS

"We'll hold the distinction of being the only nation in the history of the world that ever went to the poor house in an automobile."
WILL ROGERS

"Creditors have better memories than debtors."
BENJAMIN FRANKLIN

N ot long ago I stopped in a jewelry store to have a ring sized and was standing at the counter when I noticed a well-dressed young man purchasing a Rolex watch. A Rolex watch has become to many people—along with a Mercedes or BMW—a symbol of success. This man was purchasing a Rolex, and yet, when the sales contract was written up, I noticed the final contract price was for approximately double the listed price! I thought there must have been some mistake, but it turned out that the ultimate price of the watch doubled after accounting for the finance charge. This man had purchased the watch with $285 down and a balance payable of $235 per month. When he walked out of the store with that watch on, he was giving the impression that he could afford a Rolex. Yet the question is, could he really?

Look at the Financial Planning Diagram on page 120. In this chapter we will focus on two of the five spending areas as we discuss step 3 of the financial planning process, "How to Increase the Cash-Flow Margin."

Financial Planning Diagram

Figure 9.1

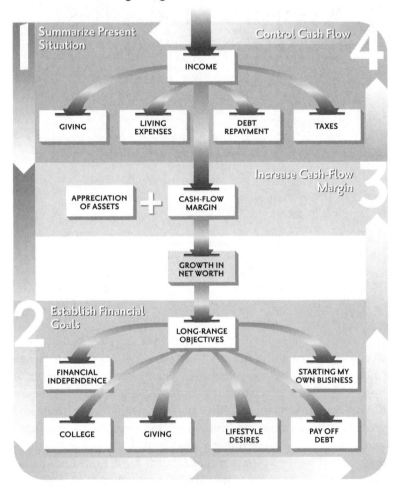

Positive Cash Flow

A positive cash-flow margin is absolutely essential if you are to accomplish either long-term or short-term financial goals. Without a cash-flow margin, you cannot save in order to meet long-term goals. In addition, each of four other short-term goals—tax reduction, increased giving, debt reduction, and increased living expense—can only be met by having a positive cash flow.

In order to reduce taxes, two things must happen: either additional expenditures must be made for such things as increased giving, IRAs, tax-exempt investments, and the like; or income must be reduced. Either increased deductible expenses or reduced income will result in tax reduction. However, both require that there be a positive cash flow to begin the process.

Without a positive cash flow, increased giving is not an option. Once there is a positive cash flow, however, and it is used to increase giving, that decision results in decreased taxes, because charitable contributions are deductible. As a financial planner, I have seen many people plan all of their tax reduction through giving. However, they had to have a cash-flow margin to begin the process.

Obviously, if you want to reduce your debt principal payments, you must have the excess cash to do so. If you are "going in the hole" by overspending as was illustrated in chapter 7, then there is no way to get out of debt until you generate a positive cash flow. After debt retirement, that extra amount can be used to reduce debt further, which in turn increases the cash flow.

Lastly, if a couple or individual has a short-term goal to increase the level of their lifestyle through a new home purchase, a new car purchase, vacations, additional gifting at Christmas, or eating out more often, they must have a positive cash flow to have the additional funds.

When you look at chart 9-A on page 122, you see that a couple earning $30,000 a year, tithing 10 percent, paying taxes at the rate of 18 percent, having no debt repayment, and spending $21,600 to live has no cash-flow margin. In order to increase their living expenses by $4,800, they must increase their income by $6,800 in order to have, after tithing 10 percent and paying taxes of $1,224, an incremental cash flow of $4,896 with which to fund the increased living expenses.

To look at this illustration another way, if this couple were earning $36,800, tithing 10 percent and paying their taxes, and if they *decreased* their lifestyle by $4,800, all of that amount would go to the bottom line—the cash-flow margin. Therefore, reducing living expenses causes a dollar-for-dollar increase in cash-flow margin;

whereas increasing living expenses requires an income increase if there is no beginning cash-flow margin equal to the increase in living expenses plus the taxes and tithe paid on that amount.

This fact is often overlooked when couples plan their expenses. They forget that to fund an increase in one area through the means of increasing income, they must also fund the taxes and tithe paid on that income. Couples deciding that a wife should work in order to have additional money available to spend often overlook this and find themselves going deeper into debt, first of all, by increasing their living expenses by the amount of the increased income, forgetting that the taxes must be paid on that increased income, not to mention the additional tithe.

The True Cost of Lifestyle

Chart 9-A

	BEFORE	AFTER	INCREASE
Income	$30,000	$36,800	$6,800
Tithe @ 10%	(3,000)	(3,680)	(680)
Taxes @ 18%	(5,400)	(6,624)	(1,224)
Debt payment	-0-	-0-	-0-
Net spendable income	21,000	26,496	4,896
Living expenses	(21,600)	(26,400)	(4,800)
CASH-FLOW MARGIN	$-0-	$96	$96

Living expenses and debt go hand in hand. Typically debt is used to fund living expenses and, conversely, without the ability to borrow, the ability to increase the lifestyle is not there. Let me repeat: debt elimination and lifestyle reduction both have a dollar-for-dollar impact on the future cash-flow margin, thereby giving the flexibility to accomplish many other goals such as tax reduction, increased giving, and savings.

Common Mistake #1: A Consumptive Lifestyle

I have been asked many times what the biggest financial mistake I see is, and the answer is easy—*a consumptive lifestyle*. A consumptive lifestyle is simply spending more than you can afford, or spending more than you should, given your other goals and priorities. Almost everyone in America falls victim to living a consumptive lifestyle. The illustration of the man purchasing the Rolex is all too common.

Because I have known many who give away substantial sums of

money, I was asked by one Christian leader what a million-dollar giver looks like. My response was, "If he looks like he can give a million dollars, he probably can't." The point is that someone whose lifestyle requires substantial expenditures must earn a considerable amount of money to have enough left after taxes to fund that lifestyle. Someone in a 40 percent tax bracket spending $100,000 to live must earn at least $166,667 to have $100,000 left after taxes to spend on that lifestyle. There is no way around that through tax planning, since tax planning requires that money be spent in order to reduce taxes.

We are, as a society, bombarded with a hedonistic philosophy.

- ❖ "Enjoy it now."
- ❖ "You only go around once."
- ❖ "Live it up."
- ❖ "You owe it to yourself."

Incidentally, I have observed—not at all scientifically proven, but still observed—that the more television a person watches, the higher lifestyle the person is apt to desire. Television advertising is extremely sophisticated and effective. In a similar way, the more time you spend in shopping malls, the higher lifestyle you are apt to want, because you are surrounding yourself with temptation. It is much like going to the grocery store just before mealtime to do your weekly shopping. Chances are that you will spend substantially more than if you went after a meal and with a specific list in hand.

Common Mistake #2: No Budget

The second most common mistake in the area of living expenses is the lack of a budget. If you have no budget, which is in effect a short-term plan, in reality you are planning to live as a responder. The best illustration of this is the person who "saves" thousands of dollars buying things on sale that are not needed. Women tend to buy responsively—hats, shoes, coats, and dresses, but the problem with being a responder is not all a female problem. Men tend to buy bigger items responsively—boats, cars, investments, and second homes.

The whole idea of living on a budget is distasteful to almost all of us because we view it as constraining. A budget can be one of the most financially freeing things you can have. A budget guides you and tells you when you are on course, just as a road map does when driving in an unfamiliar area. Not having the map creates fear, perhaps frustration, and certainly anxiety. The same can be said about living without a budget. A budget doesn't keep you from spending money on your needs and wants; it keeps you from spending responsively and unwisely.

Common Mistake #3: Driving to the Poor House

The third most common mistake in the lifestyle area occurs in buying and selling automobiles. There may be more pride and ego involved in decisions about automobiles than any other financial decisions. A quote in a newspaper points this out: "Logic and automobile purchases do not go hand in hand."

Most of the time when I have the opportunity to speak to groups, I promise to tell them before I am finished the name of the cheapest car they can own. This statement always creates a lot of interest. I learned this information several years ago before I became a Christian. Although I had achieved almost every financial goal I desired, I still wanted to purchase and drive a brand-new Cadillac. (This was before the Mercedes and BMW were status symbols.)

However, I was only thirty years old at the time and felt that driving a new Cadillac would be pretentious and might even be harmful for my business, so I purchased an Oldsmobile 98 with all the accessories. At the time, I thought that within a couple of years, "when I was older," I would trade the car in on a new Cadillac. During that time period, however, I became a Christian, and my goals and desires changed rather rapidly regarding material possessions. I lost interest in driving a new Cadillac.

As time went on, the Oldsmobile eventually had close to 150,000 miles on it—and looked it. The car had to be replaced. Once you start looking at new automobiles, your tastes change and your desires increase. I found myself looking at new cars in parking lots, on the road while I was driving, stopping at auto dealerships, and in every way lusting after a new car.

I decided at that point to do a study to determine the best car to buy from a strictly economical standpoint, taking into account all of the factors, such as gas mileage, cost of repairs, license cost, financing cost, opportunity cost of the cash paid out, insurance cost, and depreciation. I spent hours and hours comparing all the numbers and com-

Car Analysis: Keeping Old Versus Buying New

Chart 9-B

	MID-PRICED AMERICAN				AVERAGE AMERICAN				EXPENSIVE FOREIGN				INEXPENSIVE FOREIGN			
	NEW CASH	NEW FIN.	3 YR	8 YR	NEW CASH	NEW FIN.	3 YR	8 YR	NEW CASH	NEW FIN.	3 YR	8 YR	NEW CASH	NEW FIN.	3 YR	8 YR
Car cost	$15,000	$15,000	$7,500	$3,000	$10,000	$10,000	$3,500	$1,000	$25,773	$25,773	$18,000	$10,000	$5,500	$5,500	$3,100	$1,000
Gas (gallons) (1) (2)	1,500	1,500	1,500	1,500	1,350	1,350	1,350	1,350	900	900	900	900	668	668	668	668
Oil	60	60	80	100	60	60	80	100	60	60	80	100	60	60	80	100
Maintenance	—	—	300	600	—	—	300	600	—	—	300	600	—	—	300	600
Repairs	150	150	450	1,200	100	100	300	800	258	258	775	2,000	55	55	165	440
License/tax	261	261	111	24	140	140	56	15	446	446	245	70	98	98	59	17
Insurance	488	488	440	420	336	336	308	282	633	633	620	600	299	299	265	246
Principal/Int. (3)	—	4,294	—	—	—	2,862	—	—	—	7,680	—	—	—	1,574	—	—
Opportunity cost (4)	2,250	450	—	—	1,500	300	—	—	3,866	773	—	—	825	165	—	—
New car fund (5)	876	876	876	876	588	588	588	588	1,500	1,500	1,500	1,500	316	316	316	316
Depreciation	2,500	2,500	1,000	250	2,166	2,166	500	100	2,591	2,591	1,600	1,000	800	800	400	100
Annual cost	$8,085	$10,579	$4,757	$4,970	$6,240	$7,902	$3,482	$3,835	$10,254	$14,841	$6,020	$6,770	$3,121	$4,035	$2,253	$2,487

Assumptions:

(1) 15,000 miles/year: $1.50/gal.

(2) Gallon figures taken from *Consumer's Report*—combined city and highway

(3) Finance 80% of cost at 20% for three years (This figure is net of tax savings, figuring a 50% taxpayer.)

(4) Interest that could have been earned on money spent on car.

(5) Amount needed to be saved annually at 10% to buy same car in ten years.

ing up with a definite conclusion. I found without exception that the cheapest car I could own was that Oldsmobile! Even though the cost of repairs was substantial and the fuel economy was incredibly low, they did not offset the much higher costs related to a new car in terms of license, insurance, maintenance, depreciation, financing costs, or opportunity costs. Not only was I disappointed that as a CPA I could not economically justify a different car, but I was stunned at the result. I had always assumed that the low-priced, high fuel economy foreign cars would be the most economical to own.

After studying this whole issue of buying automobiles, I came to two conclusions: The cheapest car anyone can ever own is always the car *they presently own,* unless it is sold and the proceeds reinvested in a lower priced car; and the longer a car is driven, the cheaper it becomes to operate.

I did not share these results with very many people until after the *Wall Street Journal* published an article with an analysis of automobile ownership. The article stated that "the longer a car is kept (new or used), the cheaper it becomes to run per mile. . . . Average depreciation of a new car during the first year is 31.5 percent of its purchase price." The article also stated that the typical purchase price for a one-to-four-year-old used car ranges from 20 percent to 80 percent below that of a new car. Chart 9-B on page 125 compares four different types of automobiles to illustrate the two points just made—that the least expensive car you can drive is the one you presently own, and that the longer you drive an automobile, the cheaper it becomes to operate.

One of the ways, then, that living expenses can be decreased most dramatically is by merely deciding to continue driving the car you presently own. If you can also repair it and maintain it yourself, you will, over time, have substantial cash-flow savings that can be invested for the future rather than be consumed in the present.

Another *Wall Street Journal* article entitled "Riddle: Why Won't a Typical Millionaire Take You for a Ride in His Fancy Car?" reported on Thomas Stanley, a marketing professor at Georgia State University in Atlanta, who had been studying "the ways of the rich, particularly those with a net worth of at least $1 million for the past three decades." What he found, among other things, was that millionaires usually drive "four-door American sedans or Volvos with no chrome. Old vehicles are not uncommon. 'These are the most traditional people in the world,' says Mr. Stanley."

How did they become wealthy? In part by doing what we are talking about in this chapter—avoiding three of the common mistakes individuals make—having a consumptive lifestyle, not having a budget, and unnecessarily buying an automobile.

Action Points

The major key to success in reducing living expenses is recognizing that every dollar saved in the living expense category goes directly to the cash-flow margin. Each living expense item must be evaluated item by item and then controlled—there is no magical way, but each reduction frees dollars for other goals.

As an illustration, look at the living expenses of Bob and Laura on pages 91 to 93; then examine the cuts they arbitrarily decided to make in chart 9-C.

Increasing Your Margin: Bob & Laura

Chart 9-C

REDUCE LIVING EXPENSES BY:	MONTHLY AMOUNT	ANNUAL AMOUNT
Reduce Housing by:	$100	$1,200
Reduce Food by:	25	300
Reduce Transportation by:	50	600
Reduce Entertainment/Recreation by:	20	240
Reduce Insurance by:		786
Reduce Spending on the Children by:	90	1,080
Reduce Gifts by:		500
Reduce Miscellaneous by:	25	300
	TOTAL	$5,006

Some observations regarding these decisions:

1. Some areas are not cut at all because there is no ability and/ or desire to cut in that area; for example, medical expenses and clothing.

2. Many of the specific reductions come from giving up or delaying a desired consumption or purchase, such as eliminating eating out one night per month.

3. Some items undoubtedly can be cut by merely shopping better or buying more wisely, such as in the area of insurance.

4. Many ideas for reducing expenses may come from friends and others in similar financial circumstances.

5. Be careful not to reduce or eliminate an expense this year that would be more costly, perhaps, next year. This is especially true in the areas of maintenance and repairs on automobiles and homes.

6. James 1:5 says, "If any of you lacks wisdom, let him ask of God, who gives to all liberally and without reproach." God is pleased to give you creative ways to reduce your expenses when you come to Him humbly asking for His guidance and wisdom. It has been my experience that God gives unusual creativity to those who demonstrate a desire and obedience to His plans and purposes.

By merely choosing to do so, Bob and Laura were able to decrease their total annual living expenses by $5,006, which is an 18.4 percent reduction in their total living expenses. As I look at their choices, it does not appear to me that they are going to decrease their lifestyle substantially by decisions they made. However, saving $5,000 a year by consuming less will result over a long time period in an incredible amount. Remember, a dollar saved does not put a dollar, but multiple dollars, into the future.

The Mistakes of Debt

The common mistakes in financial planning are often, in one way or another, related to debt. Debt and lifestyle go hand in hand in American society. When you use debt to fund a consumptive lifestyle, not only do you have the consumptive lifestyle working against you financially, but you also have the additional burden of debt working against you financially. Both should be avoided like the plague!

The Plastic Way to Debt

Avoiding the use of debt is incredibly difficult in America's economy. The promotion of credit card use has made debt so easy to obtain and so difficult to resist the temptation. Credit card companies are spending hundreds of billions of dollars to entice each of us to spend and to use debt with cards that make spending "easier." Those billions are a pittance when compared to the additional advertising dollars of retailers.

When Sears introduced "The Discover Card," they used Atlanta as a test market. The newspaper articles at the time of its introduction reported that Sears' officials expected credit card usage to go up by $35,000,000,000 as a result of the introduction of this new card. Their studies showed that the card use would be incremental borrowing rather than replacement borrowing. In other words, people would be adding to their already existing credit card debt because the new card was nothing more than an additional line of credit for them.

I was talking with a banker friend of mine one day about credit card debt and how the banking industry viewed people who paid off their debt every month. He advised me that in the banking industry, a person who uses his or her credit card for convenience sake and pays off the debt each month is known as a "deadbeat." What a difference a few years makes! When I was growing up, a deadbeat was someone who *didn't* pay his bills; now a deadbeat is someone who does pay his bills and does it promptly! Lending institutions do not want people to pay their credit card debts each month because of the 18 to 21 percent interest that is earned on that credit card debt.

A Way Out

The *only absolute way to avoid the use of debt,* in the first place, is to have a financial plan prepared at the beginning of each year that does not allow for the use of debt. Then stick with that plan through self-discipline.

The major problem most people face is how to get out of the debt that they are already in. There are only two ways to get out of debt after making the decision to avoid the use of debt: Examine the assets you have to see which ones could be sold in order to reduce debt; and in the absence of assets to sell to eliminate debt, set up a repayment schedule and strictly adhere to it.

I once purchased a used car from a young woman who was in the process of getting a divorce from her husband. During a test drive of the car, she told me that the payments on her car, which was less than a year old, were $476 per month. This amount did not include the insurance and other ancillary costs of operation. I don't know what her annual earnings were, but $476 a month had to be a substantial portion of her monthly earnings.

She had purchased the car less than a year earlier and was now having to sell it to me for approximately two-thirds of the purchase price. In doing so, she was freeing up $476 a month or $5,712 per year in cash flow. Obviously, she will have to purchase another car, so that amount is not totally free; but she had reduced her debt by selling the assets that caused the debt.

Assets may be liquidated such as investments or savings accounts. Perhaps borrowing from the cash value of life insurance is possible at a lower interest rate than what is being paid on credit card and consumer debt.

In determining which assets to sell in order to reduce debt, remember that the assets sold should have a lower yield or appreciation rate than the debt cost. For example, in Bob and Laura's case (see page 91), if they sell the boat in order to reduce the debt, they should be able to realize $6,000, which is the listed market value on their net worth statement, and of course this $6,000 is generating no income or appreciation. In fact, it is depreciating. They could, then, use the proceeds of that sale to eliminate the boat loan of $5,000, costing $200 per month of cash flow, and save a 14 percent interest rate, which is not a bad rate of return for any investment. By eliminating the boat loan through the sale of the boat, they essentially made an investment that yielded 14 percent. They also could borrow $1,000 from their life insurance cash value.

If they sell this asset, they will eliminate all of their monthly payments, except the home mortgage, and free up $7,800 on an annual basis, or $650 on a monthly basis, which goes to reduce the negative cash-flow margin they have been facing. That $7,800 plus the $5,006 generated by reducing living expenses totals a $12,806 cash-flow increase.

However, some of their income is going to disappear from the real estate investment. That amount is $2,150, so the positive cash-flow impact of selling assets to reduce debt is $5,650 before considering the tax ramifications of so doing.

The logical question that comes up at this point is twofold. First of all, did the selling of assets to reduce debt make economic sense? Second, what impact did it have on their tax situation?

First of all, economically they have reduced high cost debt by choosing to sell low productive or nonproductive assets. Their interest paid far surpassed the increase in value on the real estate. Their debt interest paid ranged from 9 to 14 percent. The increase in value on the real estate was possibly 5 to 7 percent. Therefore, it has to make economic sense over time, and the impact on their cash flow is immediately a positive $5,650; and the impact on their net worth is neutral. There is no impact on the net worth, because a dollar reduction in assets is offset by a dollar reduction in debt.

In chapter 12 we will look at the tax impact of these decisions to determine whether they make tax sense. As a matter of fact, it does make tax sense. Even if it did not, the decision would still have been a good one because of the relieved pressure of not having to fund continually the negative cash flow and endure the anxiety and strain such a situation causes in a marriage.

Repayment—the Hard Way

Not everyone has the luxury, however, of selling assets to repay debt. Many of you are perhaps deeply in debt and have no assets at all. Many, if not most, Americans owe more than what they own; therefore, selling assets is not an option. The only option, then—other than receiving an inheritance or striking oil—is the slow, painful, and difficult process of making monthly payments. You must decide, first of all, not to take on any more debt, and second, to set up a schedule of debt repayment.

I recommend that, rather than a debt consolidation loan, you go directly to your creditor with the schedule in hand of how you are going to repay the debt, and that you do two things:

❖ Pay something on each debt each month so that the creditor knows you are serious.

❖ Concentrate on eliminating the smallest debt first. You need to have some reward quickly for a difficult project. When you have eliminated the smallest debt first, then you can apply the additional amount available from not having to pay on that debt anymore to the second smallest debt that you have, and on up the ladder. You will be building a momentum that is exciting and encouraging.

One of the other keys to repaying debt is to commit *in advance* any extra income or amounts from reduced expenses—in other words, excess cash flow—to debt repayment. This is an opportunity for you to see God work in your financial lives. He will provide funds in an unexpected and supernatural way as a result of your obedience to Him. For example, a bonus at work, a gift, additional overtime, etc. Spiritually, what you need to be asking during this time is, "God, what would You have me learn?" not, "God, why are You treating me this way?" Chances are good that God did not force you into the debt situation, but by His mercy He will enable you to climb out of that situation.

I am often asked whether couples in a heavy debt situation should tithe or not, and I have two thoughts regarding this. First of all, tithing is no more or less spiritual than debt repayment if God owns it all. However, because God does own it all, a tithe, as a priority, is a statement of your recognition that God owns it all. In other words, I don't believe it is a yes/no question; rather it is a question of what is best, relative to the individual and the circumstances. A person must, however, bear in mind the two principles: *God owns it all,* and *as a priority, giving is commanded in the Bible.* The question of whether to use tithe money to fund debt repayment is a very serious spiritual decision that can only be made with much prayer and godly counsel.

Remember, faith requires a first step without full understanding and without seeing how it is all going to work out. Getting out of debt requires elements very typical of the faith walk. In most cases for the Christian it requires faith even to take the first step.

Go with the Green

One last point on debt. Many years ago when I began thinking of financial planning as a career, I understood the importance of living on a budget. Prior to that time I used credit cards as a convenience item while I lived according to a budget. Credit cards just made record keeping easier, and because I paid the credit card statements in full each month, there was no interest cost associated with the credit cards. But then I read somewhere that the mere use of credit cards will cause a family to spend 34 percent more, regardless of whether the full statement is paid off each month or not. I found that totally unbelievable and spent a year trying to disprove it.

The only way to disprove the information was not to use credit cards and go on a straight cash payment system. So Judy and I put away our credit cards and lived strictly on cash. We paid cash for everything.

By using cash throughout the year, my spending mentality changed. It was much more difficult to pay $25 for a tank of gas using cash than if I used a credit card. (I still had that Olds 98, affectionately labeled "Old Blue.") Paying cash at the drugstore caused me, at the very least, to hesitate, and in most cases, to eliminate those impulsive purchases at the checkout counter. Paying cash for clothes caused me to think very seriously about the need for such items. Paying cash for car repairs caused me to examine whether it could be done less expensively, either by myself or at another place. Paying cash for airplane tickets while traveling caused me to think a second time about the trip I was taking.

The conclusion of the story is that after living on a straight cash budget for a year, without using credit cards at all, our living expenses decreased by 33 percent from a level I had thought was "bare bones" to begin with.

I recognize that other alternatives exist to credit cards, such as debit cards or writing checks. But my point is that there is something about parting with actual legal tender currency that helps with our discipline and decision making.

Here are the common questions I receive about this recommendation:

❖ *Isn't there a risk in carrying cash?* Of course there is. So you learn to be more cautious and plan ahead for the need for cash. I might add that the risk of overspending without planning to pay cash is greater than the loss of cash out of a purse or wallet.

❖ *Isn't it awfully inconvenient to have cash on hand at all times?* Of course it is, but the benefit of reduced spending is well worth the price paid.

❖ *Don't I need my credit cards to establish credit?* In many cases, a retailer may demand to see a credit card before accepting a check, but often a driver's license will suffice. This kind of situation is also a tremendous opportunity to share why you don't use credit cards and how God is faithful to provide for you in a superabundant way. Also, it may be an opportunity for you to share the gospel message. In chapter 1, I pointed out that the Christian will be "different," not "better." We show our difference by attempting to be nonconsumptive.

❖ *Isn't this recommendation awfully narrow-minded and restrictive?* That question is answered many times in the book of Proverbs:

He who deals with a slack hand becomes poor, but the hand of the diligent makes one rich. —Proverbs 10:4

The hand of the diligent will rule, but the slothful will be put to forced labor. —Proverbs 12:24

The slothful man does not roast what he took in hunting, but diligence is man's precious possession. —Proverbs 12:27

Dishonest money dwindles away, but he who gathers money little by little makes it grow. —Proverbs 13:11 NIV

Poverty and shame will come to him who disdains correction. —Proverbs 13:18

Enough said!

10

DESIGNING A PERSONAL
FINANCIAL PLAN

"Never spend your money before you have it."
THOMAS JEFFERSON

*"We didn't actually overspend our budget. The allocation simply
fell short of our expenditure."*
KEITH DAVIS

When I first began financial planning several years ago, I really believed there was one standard financial plan. However, I was confused about the elements of a financial plan. In other words, where did investment planning fit into the financial plan? Where did tax planning fit into a financial plan? Where did estate planning fit into a financial plan? How did life insurance affect a financial plan?

I finally came to the conclusion that a financial plan is, in reality, nothing more than a projection over a certain time period of cash inflows and cash outflows that represent the action steps a person is taking in every area of his or her life. These action steps become a road map for the future.

Once a financial plan has been determined—in other words, the action steps decided and organized into a projection—then the financial plan can be evaluated by two questions. First of all, does the plan improve the current situation? And second, does it help the person achieve the goals he or she actually has?

Review again the Financial Planning Diagram below. Step 1 gives a picture of where you are at the present, both from a net worth standpoint and from a cash flow standpoint. Step 2 summarizes where you would like to go—in other words, your future goals. Step 3 gives the primary action steps to achieve the long-term goals through increasing the cash-flow margin. Step 4 is the way you control the financial plan. Each step is positioned on the diagram beside the area involved in that step.

Financial Planning Diagram
Figure 10.1

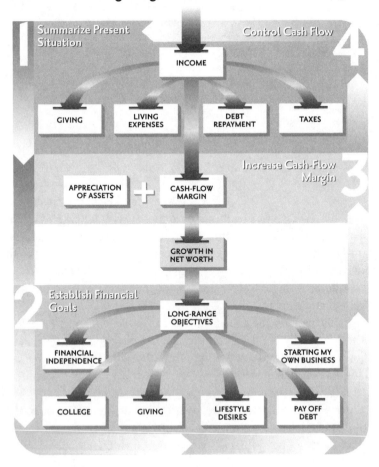

Bob and Laura's cash flow decisions (step 3 of the process) are summarized on pages 137 and 138.

The summary of all the decisions they made is a net increase in cash flow of $6,846. It came from reducing their living expenses by $5,006, reducing their debt outflow through the sale of assets by $5,400, reducing their tax withholding by $1,000 (because of lower taxes due to increased giving; this will be explained in chapter 12), and decreasing their investment income through the sale of certain assets.

Those action steps are then summarized into an analysis of their cash flow, both "Before Planning" and "After Planning" as depicted in Chart 10-B. Their financial plan is comprised of the action steps taken in the right-hand column and is literally the "After Planning" summary of their cash inflows and cash outflows.

Notice that they have a net positive cash flow of $182 compared to a preplanning negative cash flow of $6,664. They have done nothing more than decide to go from a negative cash flow to a positive cash flow by adopting a less consumptive lifestyle and by choosing to eliminate their debt by selling certain assets. Now that they are generating a cash-flow margin, Bob and Laura can begin to accomplish their long-term goals.

Increasing Your Margin: Bob & Laura   Chart 10-A

	MONTHLY AMOUNT	ANNUAL AMOUNT
REDUCE LIVING EXPENSES BY:		
Reduce Housing by:	$100	$1,200
Reduce Food by:	25	300
Reduce Transportation by:	50	600
Reduce Entertainment/Recreation by:	20	240
Reduce Insurance by:		786
Reduce Spending on the Children by:	90	1,080
Reduce Gifts by:		500
Reduce Miscellaneous by:	25	300
TOTAL	310	5,006
REDUCE TOTAL DEBT BY:		
Sell boat	$200	$2,400
Borrow $1,000 from insurance		
Sell real estate	200	2,400

		50	600
Pay off credit cards			
	TOTAL	$450	$5,400
REDUCE TOTAL TAXES BY:			
Change W-4 to reduce withholding by $1,000			$1,000
	TOTAL		$1,000
RESTRUCTURE TOTAL INVESTMENTS BY:			
Sell real estate			(2,000)
	TOTAL		(2,000)
	MARGIN INCREASE		$9,406
	INCREASE IN GIVING		(2,560)
	TOTAL MARGIN INCREASE		$6,846

Cash Flow Analysis Summary: Bob & Laura   Chart 10-B

	BEFORE PLANNING	AFTER PLANNING	ACTION STEPS
INCOME:			
	$49,600	$47,600	
LESS:			
Giving	2,200	4,760	Write Giving check before paying other bills.
Taxes	10,014	9,014	Increase withholding allowances and reduce amount withheld.
Debt	8,556	3,156	Sell assets and pay off debt except mortgage and car.
Total Priority Expenses	20,770	16,930	
Net Spendable Income	$28,830	$30,670	
LIVING EXPENSES:			
Housing	$12,608	$11,408	Reduce by $100/month.
Food	4,800	4,500	Reduce $25/month.
Clothing	1,000	1,000	
Transportation	2,660	2,060	Reduce $50/month by shopping for auto insurance; do maintenance at home.
Entertainment/recreation	2,140	1,900	Reduce $20/month.
Medical	1,260	1,260	
Insurance	1,536	750	Cancel policies with debt; replace with $100,000 term insurance.
Children	6,960	5,880	Reduce $90/month.
Gifts	1,150	650	Make some gifts; plan ahead; shop sales.
Miscellaneous	1,380	1,080	Reduce $25/month.
TOTAL	$35,494	$30,488	
CASH-FLOW MARGIN	($6,664)	$182	

Balance Sheet Analysis Summary: Bob & Laura   Chart 10-C

	BEFORE PLANNING	AFTER PLANNING	ACTION STEPS
ASSETS			
Cash	$2,000	$2,000	Invest in money market fund.
Savings	1,000	1,500	Cash from sale of assets
Market securities	-0-	-0-	
Life insurance: cash values	6,000	-0-	Borrow cash value, cancel policies with loans.
Home	112,000	112,000	
Boat	6,000	-0-	Sell and pay off debt.
Automobile	8,000	8,000	
Furniture	5,000	5,000	
Real estate investments	15,000	-0-	Sell and pay off debt.
TOTAL ASSETS	$155,000	$128,500	
LIABILITIES			
Charge cards	$3,000	-0-	
Installment loans	-0-	-0-	
Auto loan	6,000	6,000	
Debt to relatives	5,000	5,000	
Mortgage	81,500	81,500	
Boat loan	5,000	-0-	
Bank loans	13,500	-0-	
Life insurance loan	5,000	-0-	
TOTAL LIABILITIES	$119,000	$92,500	
NET WORTH	$36,000	$36,000	

In reality, their final financial plan will probably have one more element, since they must decide what to do with the positive cash-flow margin of $182. Their plan is certainly not a comfortable one, since there is very little margin for error. However, it is far better than the financial plan they were operating under.

The plan they now have represents the reality of their financial situation. Basically, they could not afford the lifestyle they had adopted, and they were violating a biblical principle by presuming upon the future through the acquisition of debt, probably assuming that they were going to have an increasing income with which to pay off the debt. Even if you eventually have increased income, do you want to have it all spent when it finally comes? That takes the morale out of the raise! Not to mention the defeating feeling of paying interest.

Now that their financial plan is in place, we will evaluate it, first of all, in light of its impact on the statement of net worth, because that one summary statement measures whether a person is making progress or not. Chart 10-C is a comparison of their statement of net worth before planning and after planning.

The primary thing to notice is that their net worth did not change, even though they sold $27,000 of investments and assets in order to reduce debt. Basically, they had accumulated assets beyond their ability to save in the future. Therefore, they chose to sell the assets they could not afford in order to pay the debt. This, in turn, increased their cash-flow situation to such an extent that they are now in a much stronger financial position than they were before.

The plan must also be evaluated by the second question, does the personal financial plan move Bob and Laura toward the achievement of their long-term goals?

In light of their goals in the Giving area, they have increased their giving to a 10 percent tithe, and they could also choose to give $2,000 for the new chapel at their church by taking the money out of their checking and/or savings account. Of course, that would mean giving up the emergency fund and flexibility factor in their financial situation, but that is not to say it would not be a wise spiritual decision. The decision depends upon the prayerfully determined goals that God has given them. At least they can measure the impact of whatever financial decisions they make on their situation.

They are not making progress toward the goal of funding college education except to the extent that they can generate a positive cash flow and eventually repay debt. As they do, each year the funds can be allocated more and more to this high priority goal.

A cash-flow margin will also make it possible for Bob and Laura to achieve some of their major lifestyle desires such as replacing Laura's car, and they may choose to use savings account balances or checking account balances to accomplish some of these objectives. The reductions in their living expenses, especially in such areas as Entertainment and Gifts, may make them feel they are giving up the one goal of maintaining their present lifestyle in order to accomplish some other goals. However, that's a personal evaluation. My evaluation is that their lifestyle will not be appreciably hurt.

One of their major objectives is to pay off debt, and all debt will be paid for under this financial plan with the exception of the home mortgage, the car debt, and the debt to parents.

They also indicated they would like to have $5,000 invested in a money market fund. This is one of the action steps that they can— and should—take as part of their written financial plan. Therefore, they will accomplish this goal. In addition, they would like to pass on to their children at least $100,000. Their net worth of $36,000 is a step toward the accomplishment of that goal and has not been reduced by the financial plan they are putting into place.

The only thing left for Bob and Laura to do at this point is to *take* the action steps they have decided on. Until they do so, they have not exercised faith, for faith without works is dead, and plans without action are mere talk.

Vision for the Future: Bob & Laura   Chart 10-D

In five years, we see the following taking place:

GIVING	
☒ We would be giving 10% per year.	
☐ We would be making additional gifts each year of:	
☒ We would have made total gifts of:	$2,000 for the new chapel

COLLEGE			
☒ A college fund would exist for each of our children:			
Child	Type of College	Approximate Annual Cost	Total Cost
Sue	State college	$6,000	$24,000

LIFESTYLE DESIRES	
☒ We would have made the following major purchases: (new home, car, vacations, etc.)	
Item	Amount
Replace Laura's car	$5,000
Redecorate living room	$5,000
Buy a new house	$20,000
☒ We would have the following type of lifestyle: (increase, decrease, or maintain present level)	
Maintain our present lifestyle.	

PAY OFF DEBT	
We would have paid off the following debts:	
Owed to	**Total**
Credit cards	$3,000
Boat loan	5,000
Bank loan	13,500
Parents' loan	5,000
Auto loan	6,000
Life insurance	5,000

BEGIN BUSINESS
We will have started our own business, which will require an investment of:

FINANCIAL INDEPENDENCE		
We will have the following investments:		
Type of Investmetn	**Amount Invested**	**Annual Return**
Emergency fund	$5,000	$5,000
I would like to pass on to my spouse (children) the following estate:		
$100,000		
We will have the adequate investment income to support our lifestyle of:	$	per month

Faith will always require an action step. Once the action steps have been taken and the financial plan is thus in place and working, they will need to control the living expenses—to carry out step 4 of the financial planning process.

Again, I want to emphasize that *financial planning is a process.* Circumstances will change throughout the years, goals will change, and desires will change. We live in a dynamic environment, and flexibility is one aspect of a financial plan. Generally, I recommend that a financial plan be reviewed at least on an annual basis and, in the earlier years of developing the discipline of financial planning, that it be reviewed and perhaps revised on a quarterly basis. As time goes on, you will find that the process of financial planning becomes almost automatic as you implement the principles and put them into practice.

Use the following pages to design your own financial plan and evaluate its impact on your statement of net worth. We are now at the "perspiration point" of financial planning. However, it is also the most exciting point, because you can discover the action steps needed to achieve your real goals and to incorporate biblical principles into your daily life.

Increasing Your Margin

Chart 10-E

	MONTHLY AMOUNT	ANNUAL AMOUNT
REDUCE LIVING EXPENSES BY:		
REDUCE TOTAL DEBT BY:		
REDUCE TOTAL TAXES BY:		
RESTRUCTURE TOTAL INVESTMENTS BY:		
TOTAL		
MARGIN INCREASE		
INCREASE IN GIVING		
TOTAL MARGIN INCREASE		

Your Cash Flow Analysis Summary

Chart 10-F

	BEFORE PLANNING	AFTER PLANNING	ACTION STEPS
INCOME:			
LESS:			
Giving			
Taxes			
Debt			
Total Priority Expenses			
Net Spendable Income			
LIVING EXPENSES:			
Housing			
Food			
Clothing			
Transportation			
Entertainment/recreation			
Medical			
Insurance			
Children			
Gifts			
Miscellaneous			
TOTAL			
CASH-FLOW MARGIN			

Your Net Worth Analysis Summary

Chart 10-G

	BEFORE PLANNING	AFTER PLANNING	ACTION STEPS
ASSETS			
TOTAL ASSETS			

LIABILITIES			
TOTAL LIABILITIES			
NET WORTH			

11

CONTROL THE FLOW

> *"O money, money, money, I'm not necessarily one of those who thinks thee holy,*
> *but I often stop to wonder how thou canst go out so fast when thou comest in so slowly."*
> OGDEN NASH

> *"Fools can make money. It takes a wise man to know how to spend it."*
> ENGLISH PROVERB

Many people tell me stories about the cookie jar where Grandpa and Grandma used to keep all of their cash. As income was earned, it went into the cookie jar. As needs arose, the money to pay for them was taken out of the cookie jar. When the cookie jar was empty, there was no more spending until more cash was received.

As time went on and the management of expenses became more complex for our grandparents, they gave up the cookie jar and started to use an envelope system. Money was placed in various envelopes according to the allocations of the income—one envelope for food, one envelope for clothes, one envelope for giving, and one envelope for insurance, depending on how many allocations they wanted to have. But the cookie jar principle still applied. The income was allocated and placed into the envelopes, and money was spent in the various areas allotted. When an envelope was empty, the spending stopped until more cash was received and placed in it.

In examining the cookie jar or envelope system, we find *three basic principles* that were applied in order to control cash flow. The first principle is that money was always allocated. Every dollar was told where to go. In the era of the cookie jar, the inflow and the outgo were so closely related that it was not necessary to allocate to various categories. The spending was done as the need arose. However, as both income and kinds of expenses increased, the income had to be allocated and placed in an envelope for the intended use.

Financial Planning Diagram

Figure II.I

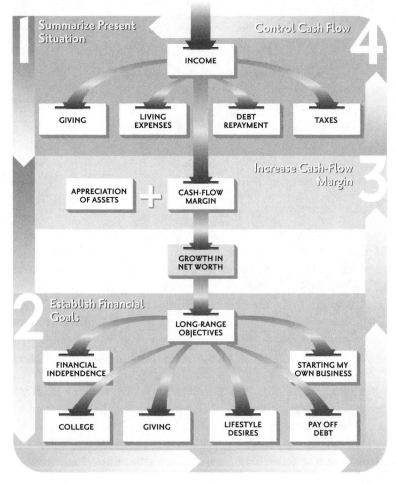

The second principle is that spending always stopped when the envelope or cookie jar was empty. The reason was simple—there were no alternatives. The absence of cash was the surest form of control.

A third principle is that the individuals always had a current awareness of the financial situation relative to the planned situation. It was very simple to determine whether there was any money left in the envelope or the cookie jar. If there was, not all of the spending had been done that the plan called for. If, on the other hand, it was empty, the plan had been accomplished.

The same guiding principles need to be evident in any cash-flow control system: an allocation of income, an end to spending when the spending limit is reached, and a current awareness of the financial situation relative to the plan.

Cash-Flow Control Process

In order to put a cash-flow control system in place, you must accomplish five steps. I want to caution you that this five-step process may take as much as two years to accomplish, and *it is essential that there be flexibility.* A budget—and I have avoided using that word as much as possible, but that is in effect what we are discussing—is never the law, but rather a guide.

The process is as follows:

Step 1: Estimate your living expenses.

Using chart 7-R, Exhibit E on pages 100 and 101, estimate your living expenses in as much detail as possible. I suggest that you not attempt to estimate them down to the penny, but rather shoot for 80 percent accuracy in your first attempt.

Step 2: Record what actually happens.

At this point in the process, you are capturing the data in order to evaluate how closely your actual expenses are to what you estimated them to be. (Recording the data and increasing your awareness also help you control your spending.) You will need a system of summarizing all of your expenses according to the expense categories you previously estimated. You can do this on worksheets or on your computer with money management software.

Step 3: Establish a budget.

After you have estimated your expenses and recorded what has actually happened over a time period of three to twelve months, it is time to establish a budget. Perhaps you will want to use the percentage guide in chart 11-A below for setting up your own budget.

Your Family Income Percentage Guide   Chart II-A

All percentages are of gross income.

Gross Income	$25,000	$35,000	$45,000	$55,000	$65,000	DOLLARS	PERCENT
Tithe	10%	10%	10%	10%	10%	$	%
Taxes	13%	19%	20%	21%	25%		
Debt	0%	0%	0%	0%	0%		
Total Priority Expenses	23%	29%	30%	31%	35%		
Net Spendable Income	77%	71%	70%	69%	65%		
Living Expenses							
Housing	29%	24%	21%	19%	17%		
Food	9%	9%	8%	8%	7%		
Clothing	4%	4%	4%	4%	4%		
Transportation	12%	9%	8%	8%	7%		
Entertainment/recreation	4%	4%	4%	5%	5%		
Medical	4%	3%	3%	3%	3%		
Insurance	4%	4%	4%	3%	3%		
Children	2%	2%	2%	2%	2%		
Gifts	1%	1%	1%	1%	1%		
Miscellaneous	4%	5%	7%	7%	7%		
Total Living Expenses	73%	65%	62%	60%	56%		
Margin	4%	6%	8%	9%	9%		

ASSUMPTIONS:

1. Figures are based on a family of four and are provided as a guide only. Your personal circumstances may necessitate different allocations.
2. The tax percentages assume that the standard deduction is taken.
3. There is no consumer debt.
4. Margin can be used for other expenses (private education, etc.).

Step 4: Control the budget.

Almost any system can be used. Many couples I know still use the basic envelope system to control their budget. They put an allocated amount of money each month into various envelopes and stop spending when the envelope is empty.

Another alternative is a sheet of paper for each allocated spending category. List on the sheet of paper the date, the purpose, the deposit, the withdrawal, and the balance for that expense category just as you would in a checkbook ledger.

A more sophisticated system that I recommend for many of my clients is one that uses checkbook-type ledgers for each category and each deposit made in place of the envelopes. I recommend this system because we are accustomed to using checkbooks and recording checks as they are written, and because the checkbook ledger serves in the same way as the envelope but provides a better record of expenses. Computer financial programs are an excellent way to set up and track your family finances.

An overview of the cash control system using checkbook ledgers is depicted in figure 11.2.

Incorporating Principles into Your Budget

The cash-flow control system should allow the incorporation of several basic principles.

❖ *Assigned accountability.* Husband and wife each have areas of budget responsibility. For example, the husband may be responsible for mortgage and utility payments while the wife is responsible for food and miscellaneous spending. Each is assigned the cash allocations necessary to fulfill these functions. Also, if you notice some areas are harder to control, such as gifts or clothing, decide together who should have responsibility. If the wife is responsible and consistently struggles to stay within allotments, perhaps she will have guilt and anxiety, and the husband should take that over for a time. But it could be that the husband has responsibility and is holding too tightly to the purse strings to "prove" her fortitude, and it is causing exasperation and feelings of defeat on her part. Keep an open communication during this process and be team players as much as possible.

❖ *Immediate feedback on how actual spending measures against planned spending.* The key is to know as soon as possible when budget limits have been reached. You may feel embarrassed that you have overspent—again! But hiding this information will only compound the problem. You're in this as a team. Both of you will make mistakes. Give each other

Cash Control Overview

Figure II.2

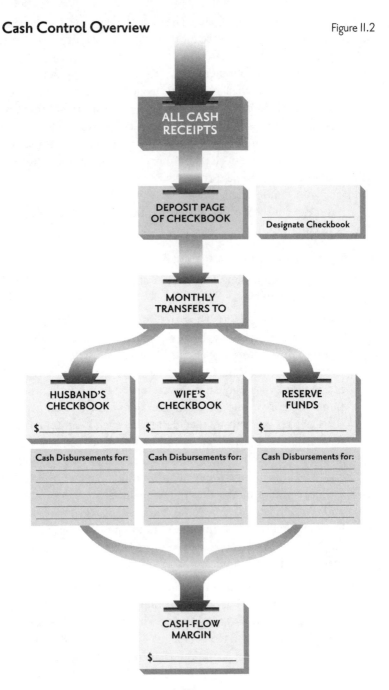

grace and muster up courage to try again—that's the only way progress is made.

❖ *Consistent discipline.* Is a budget extra work? You bet it is. However, once the budget is established, it should not require more than twenty to thirty minutes over an entire week, and the benefits are more than worth the effort.

❖ *Strict limitation of credit card use.* Nothing will destroy a budget faster than having to meet unexpected debt payments. Use credit cards only as a check (a debit or cash card) that requires a prompt accounting within the budget. But remember, even with this type of usage, you may be tempted to spend on something you'll regret later or to overspend.

❖ *Regular accumulation of all cash-flow margin.* All funds not used during the month are transferred to savings. It will be necessary during some months to transfer from savings back into the budget. For example, if you divide your property taxes into twelve equal payments and pay them to yourself monthly, move it into savings so you won't spend it! But don't forget to transfer it back to the checking when the bill comes due.

❖ *Flexibility.* At times it may be necessary to use funds allocated for one purpose for some other purpose. This can be done, but it requires a specific decision each time a transfer is made. For example, you may decide to give up entertainment money to buy clothes. The budget allows you to do this in a visible manner.

❖ *Saving ahead of time for the budget busters.* Every month or every paycheck, some amount should be set aside in a savings or separate checking account for the expenses that will occur on an other than monthly or even planned basis. Vacation, gifts, insurance payments, car repairs, and seasonal clothing are all examples of this type of expense. Chart 11-B is an example of how Bob and Laura decided to plan for their expenses.

Fixed Annual Expenses: Bob & Laura

Chart II-B

Projected, as of January 1

	WHEN PAID	ANNUAL AMOUNT	ANNUAL DIVIDED BY 12	MONTHS SINCE PAID	BEGINNING BALANCE NEEDED
Home insurance	8/1	$400	$33	5.0	$165
Property tax	10/15	1,000	83	2.5	208
Life insurance					
Medical insurance					
Disability insurance					
Auto insurance	6/1	500	42	7.0	294
Other insurance					
Other insurance					
Other taxes					
Dues: Racquet club	9/15	300	25	3.5	88
Dues:					
School tuition	8/1	6,000	500	5.0	2,500
Other: Vacation	7/1	1,000	83	6.0	498
Other: Clothing	Varies	1,000	83		
Other: Gifts	Varies	1,150	96		
Other:					
TOTAL		$11,350			$3,753
Monthly Payment to Reserve Fund			$945		

Questions and Answers on Cash-Flow Control

1. **Question:** How many category ledgers can I have?

   Answer: All you want. But remember, the more ledgers you have, the more cumbersome the system becomes. You may want to start with several to make sure you have control of each area of spending. As you become familiar with how the system works and disciplined to living within your allocations, you may want to simplify by combining several ledgers into one.

   The overall admonition is: KEEP IT SIMPLE.

2. **Question:** How do I balance my checkbook with all these ledgers and both husband and wife writing checks?

   Answer: It is really no different than balancing with one checkbook except that the balances in the different ledgers must be considered. Deposits on the bank statement have to be reconciled with the Deposits Ledger. Each cancelled check has to be reconciled with the husband's or wife's checkbook just as you normally do with one checkbook.

3. **Question:** What if I use a credit card for a purchase?

Answer: Transfer funds from the appropriate ledger into the Debt Ledger. Then when the bill arrives, the funds will be available to pay it and avoid interest charges. If the funds are not available to transfer to the Debt Ledger, then the use of credit cards is wrong.

4. **Question:** What if I make a purchase with a debit card?

Answer: Although a debit card is used at the checkout just as a credit card is used, the transaction is treated the same as writing a check. Instead of being billed for the purchase, the purchase amount will be deducted from your checking account. Since it is the same as a check, an entry for this amount should be made in your Check Ledger as soon as possible. A debit card is a good cash-flow control tool and is recommended over the credit card. VISA and MasterCard banks can supply debit cards.

5. **Question:** Can I use my margin for special purchases?

Answer: You can use the margin for any purpose you desire— *but* remember that the reason for generating margin is to meet long-range goals and priorities. If you use the margin today, you give up the opportunity to meet long-range goals tomorrow.

6. **Question:** I am paid on a commission-only basis, so my income is variable. How do I handle this?

Answer: Keep in mind that only a fixed amount of money is allocated to living expenses each month. All funds are deposited into the checking account and accounted for in the Deposits Ledger. In high commission periods a surplus should develop, which should supply funds during low (or no) commission periods. Obviously the easier way to start the budget is during a high (income greater than expenses) period. But don't set your budget to consume your entire current income. Set it for a conservative average.

7. **Question:** I am self-employed. Will the budget work for me?

Answer: It works the same for both employed people and those with variable incomes. You may need an additional ledger to account for self-employment taxes and for federal and state withholding taxes. Each time a deposit is made, then the transfer of an appropriate percentage for taxes should be made to a Tax Ledger. This is an untouchable ledger; that is, this money is not available for transfer for any other purposes. If you do not have the discipline *not* to spend tax money, then open a separate savings account to hold these funds.

8. **Question:** I like to keep some cash when I deposit my paycheck. How do I account for this in the budget?

   Answer: What is the cash for? That's the chief issue. If you keep cash, then simply account for it by reducing the amount transferred from the Deposits Ledger to the appropriate ledger. For example, the husband keeps $50 for gasoline and miscellaneous cash. Then he would reduce the amount that is allocated to his checkbook by $50. If the wife uses cash for dry cleaning or postage stamps, then she would record those expenditures and note to herself that cash is to be used for those purposes only. If it is spent on something else—eating out or buying something from a schoolchild's fundraiser—you must go back and change which category the cash came from. Sticky notes on cash are great reminders of how much is for which items!

9. **Question:** I have some annual expenses coming due but do not have the cash available to meet them *and* the needed household expenses. How can I start the budget?

   Answer: The ideal way to start a budget is to have a lump sum of money available for annual expenses. If we start the budget with $2,000 available, during the year we would dip into the $2,000. By the end of the year we would have recovered through regular annual expense allocations and still have $2,000. For example— car insurance immediately due ($900)—re-save and re-place.

10. **Question:** I did not see any place in the budget for furniture, home furnishings, improvements, or appliance replacement. Where are these covered?

    Answer: These are major items, and their purchase is made as a discretionary use of margin or savings. Until you have gotten spending on low-dollar items under control, I strongly recommend not purchasing high-dollar items unless absolutely necessary, and then shop wisely and do not choose the most expensive selections.

Step 5: Evaluate and revise.

Once you have been operating on a budget (the system described or your own), you need to evaluate and revise the budget periodically. This should be done at least on an annual basis, but more frequent revisions may be required as you are beginning. In my own experience, I have found that it does not take more than about two or three hours per year to set up a new budget and, on a monthly basis, twenty to thirty minutes to determine where I am relative to my financial plan. It's an exciting time! Well, maybe I am overstating it a bit. After all, I am one of those financial nerds. But it is exciting how God opens doors simply through the exercise of self-control and wisdom. It tells me a lot about how I am doing as a steward of God's resources.

12

TAX PLANNING

"I'm proud to be paying taxes in the United States. The only thing is—I could be just as proud for half the money."
ARTHUR GODFREY

"Unquestionably, there is progress. The average American now pays out twice as much in taxes as he formerly got in wages."
H. L. MENCKEN

"The hardest thing in the world to understand is the income tax."
ALBERT EINSTEIN

"The avoidance of taxes is the only intellectual pursuit that carries any reward."
JOHN MAYNARD KEYNES

I f there is one cash outflow that everyone is eager to reduce, it is income taxes.

Someone once asked me to help him plan to pay zero taxes. He was a professional who earned a very good income, and yet he was adamant that he did not want to pay taxes. He did not agree with the way the government spent his money. I was tempted to ask him whether he would like to give up his automobile—because the road system would not be maintained without taxes—or whether he could sleep at night with no military forces to protect him, and whether he would like not to have national parks to visit.

I am in no way proposing that we should pay more than we rightfully owe in taxes. There is a big difference, however, between *tax avoidance* and *tax evasion*. Tax evasion results in a jail sentence; tax avoidance results in lower taxes, but it almost never results in zero taxes. Tax avoidance is planning wisely and prudently to pay a *fair share* of taxes, but no more than what is legally owed.

I have often reflected on our attitude toward taxes and asked myself the question, why is it that we detest paying taxes? I believe the answer is multifaceted, but the primary reason is that we get no perceived benefit from paying taxes. Only in this area of our finances do we feel that once the money is gone, it seems to be gone forever. For the salaried and those living on a fixed income, fewer tax planning opportunities exist compared to those who are self-employed or own businesses with the opportunity and ability to use various tax planning tools and techniques.

When I was a practicing CPA, I prepared hundreds of tax returns each year and was asked hundreds of times over the course of several years, "How can I reduce my taxes?" I had a facetious answer for that question: "It's easy to reduce your taxes—just reduce your income." It's a guaranteed way to reduce taxes, and there is no risk to it. The point is that if your taxes are going up, your income is also going up. Taxes need to be put into proper perspective, and the proper perspective is that income taxes are levied only when there is income earned. Also, though we may see waste and inappropriate use of some tax dollars, many are spent for services we use. We are not "entitled" to those services for free. If we use them, we must pay for them. Entitlement is definitely an attitude bred by our have-it-all culture, not by God. Check your perspective and thank God for your government.

The second guaranteed way to reduce taxes is to spend more money on deductible items, such as charitable contributions, medical bills, mortgage interest, and IRA/401(k) contributions. As I pointed out in an earlier chapter, there is no such thing as a free tax deduction. If you are in the 15 percent tax bracket, then a dollar spent on a deductible item costs you eighty-five cents cash out of pocket. True, it reduces your taxes, but there has been a cost to it. I can state unequivocally that there is no free tax deduction anywhere, at any time, for anything! When you read or hear of persons who pay no taxes or who pay low taxes and have huge incomes, that may be true in the short term because of their high deductions, but those deductions have to be paid for at some time. Here are some guiding principles for tax deductions:

><><><><><><><><><><><><><><><><><><><><><><><><><><><><><><

Don't ever expect to get a free tax deduction, and never make a financial decision on the basis of its tax deductibility.

><><><><><><><><><><><><><><><><><><><><><><><><><><><><><><

It's easy for a tax accountant to make the client happy by having him overpay on withholdings and quarterly tax estimates during the year so that he always gets a refund. I don't believe this is ethical, and it certainly does not make good economic sense. My general rule for this area is:

><><><><><><><><><><><><><><><><><><><><><><><><><><><><><><

Getting a large refund check is a sign of poor stewardship.

><><><><><><><><><><><><><><><><><><><><><><><><><><><><><><

A refund check means that the taxpayer has planned poorly. The United States government does not require anyone to pay in tax withholding or quarterly estimates any more than what the taxpayer has determined the actual liability will be. I know that these preceding general principles may be difficult to deal with personally, because they go against the grain of everything you thought, and perhaps even the way you have planned. For example, many people plan to have that refund check in order to make major purchases each year. What they are really doing is admitting they do not have the discipline to save for that major purchase. You will gain more in interest if you learn to save that money little by little each month from a more accurate withholding. Please remember that tax planning does not have to be a mystery or even very difficult, especially if you understand the above two principles.

Scriptural Insights on Taxes

I have been looking in the Bible for the verse that says, "Thou shalt not pay any taxes." Unfortunately, I haven't been able to find it; nor have I been able to find a verse that tells me exactly how much I should pay in income taxes. However, I do find many principles throughout Scripture that directly apply to income taxes.

> Dishonest money dwindles away, but he who gathers money little by little makes it grow. —Proverbs 13:11 NIV

> Plans fail for lack of counsel, but with many advisers they succeed. —Proverbs 15:22 NIV

In the same way, let your light shine before men, that they may see your good deeds and praise your Father in heaven.—Matthew 5:16 NIV

Whoever can be trusted with very little can also be trusted with much, and whoever is dishonest with very little will also be dishonest with much. —Luke 16:10 NIV

Is it lawful for us to pay taxes to Caesar, or not? . . .[Jesus said to them], "Show Me a denarius. Whose portrait and inscription are on it?" "Caesar's," they replied. He said to them, "Then give to Caesar what is Caesar's, and to God what is God's." —Luke 20:22–25 NIV

Give everyone what you owe him: If you owe taxes, pay taxes: if revenue, then revenue; if respect, then respect; if honor, then honor. —Romans 13:7 NIV

Rather, we have renounced secret and shameful ways; we do not use deception, nor do we distort the word of God. On the contrary, by setting forth the truth plainly we commend ourselves to every man's conscience in the sight of God —2 Corinthians 4:2 NIV

Let me summarize these verses for you:

❖ You are called to be salt and light to a dying world. One of the ways that you are salt and light is by your good stewardship, which will require paying taxes.

❖ Your choice is fraud or faithfulness. You may reduce taxes by illegal or questionable means, but faithfulness requires you to use good planning and honesty to reduce taxes or to pay the full amount without begrudging where no deductions can be taken. Your objective is faithfulness—not tax reduction. It is God's money; He doesn't resent that you have to use it for that purpose; why should you?

❖ Some taxes are certainly due because our government has supplied services. Quite frankly, the freedoms and protection we enjoy in the United States are unparalleled anywhere in the world, and I believe that we all have a part in paying for these privileges. (I am not endorsing wastefulness and poor decisions on the part of our government, but the way to change that is through changing our representation in Congress, not through refusal to pay what is lawfully owed.)

❖ Be a planner—not a responder. It is especially important to plan in the tax area because of the many types of taxes you have.

Types of Taxes

It has been rightly said that you are taxed when you earn, you are taxed when you spend, you are taxed when you use your phone, you are taxed when your investments do well, and you are taxed when you die. As a matter of fact, you are taxed almost anytime there is a money transaction.

Some of the many kinds of taxes that you pay are:

Income taxes—Federal, state, city, and county taxes on income earned.

Sales taxes—Taxes imposed by state and local communities on sales of all types of goods and services sold.

Intangible taxes—Taxes on various intangible properties owned, usually including stocks, bonds, and other investments. State governments generally impose this tax.

Use taxes—Taxes for the use of goods and services provided by taxing authorities, such as gasoline taxes for the use of roads and airport taxes for the use of airports.

Estate taxes—Taxes imposed by the federal government on the accumulation of material wealth when a person dies.

Inheritance taxes—Taxes imposed by state and local governments, again, on estates accumulated.

Gift taxes—Taxes imposed on the transfer of various kinds of property to another person. Gift taxes and estate taxes are typically referred to as transfer taxes. In other words, the transferring of property from one person to another may result in a tax.

Property taxes—Taxes imposed by local authorities on property owned.

Social Security and Medicare taxes—Taxes imposed by the federal government on wages, earnings, and self-employment income to pay for Social Security and Medicare benefits.

This list is not meant to be all-inclusive, but merely to illustrate that you do pay taxes at almost every turn of your financial life. In this chapter I will discuss tax planning in the area of income taxes at the state and federal levels only. In chapter 14, I will deal with estate taxes. None of the other taxes will be covered in this book, because they are difficult to control, except as they relate to other spending decisions.

Income Tax Rates

Two terms must be understood before we discuss tax planning: marginal tax rates and effective tax rates or, stated another way, marginal tax brackets and effective tax brackets. When people say they are in a 15 percent tax bracket, they mean that their next dollar of income is taxed at the 15 percent level or, conversely, that their next dollar of tax deduction reduces taxes by fifteen cents.

The graduated income tax system in the United States means that various levels of income are taxed at different rates. As the income reaches a higher level, the rate goes up, but, and this is important to remember, *the rate does not go up on all of the previously earned and taxed income*—it only applies to that next dollar of income. For illustrative purposes I have constructed a hypothetical tax table as follows:

Hypothetical Tax Table
Chart 12-A

1. IF TAXABLE INCOME IS AT LEAST	2. TAX ON COLUMN 1	3. TAX ON EXCESS (ABOVE AMOUNT IN COLUMN 1)
$10,000	$1,000	12%
20,000	2,200	15%
30,000	3,700	20%
40,000	5,700	30%
50,000	8,700	40%
60,000	12,700	50%

The illustration is clearer when we define some terms.

Taxable Income. Taxable income is the portion of your earned income that is ultimately taxed after taking into account all deductions, exemptions, and other reductions due to investments, IRAs and the like. Column 3 gives the tax bracket, and it is the percentage applied to the *last* dollar of taxable income. In other words, if the taxable income in this illustration is anyplace between $10,001 and $20,000, the tax bracket is 12 percent, the percent paid on the last dollar of income.

Marginal Rate. This determines the amount that will be paid on the *next* dollar of income that cannot be offset with a deduction. If a person currently has taxable income of $30,000 and he earns one more dollar of income, that dollar of income is taxed at 20 percent.

Therefore, his marginal rate is 20 percent, and that stays 20 percent until his taxable income reaches $40,001, at which time the marginal rate to be paid goes to 30 percent. The marginal rate and the tax bracket could be the same, but won't always be. The tax bracket is determined by the *last dollar* of the taxable income, and the marginal rate is determined by the *next dollar* of taxable income. The bar chart on page 166 illustrates how the maximum marginal tax rate has changed over time. Note how low the marginal rate is as we enter the 2000s relative to other time periods. The first thing to realize is that the lower the marginal rate, the less tax-motivated any financial decision should be. Second, be on guard, because marginal tax rates can be (and will be) changed at the whim of Congress. What's true today regarding wise tax planning may not be true next year.

Effective Rate. This is the total amount paid in taxes divided by the total income earned. In the case of Bob and Laura, they earned $49,600 last year. However, they were allowed exemptions for themselves and their children, as well as itemized deductions for medical expenses, property taxes, state income taxes, and charitable contributions. All of these deductions and exemptions reduce the total income down to the taxable income. The income taxes are then computed on taxable income.

If we assume that their taxable income was $40,000, then the taxes that they would pay on the $40,000 is $5,700, which represents 11.5 percent of the total income of $49,600. Therefore, we can say that even though they are in the 20 percent tax bracket and will marginally pay 30 percent, they are effectively paying only 11.5 percent of their income in taxes. *The effective rate is the key number.* It is much more important than the tax bracket or marginal rate.

The simple objective in tax planning is to reduce the effective tax rate in order to generate after-tax dollars for any goals that you have.

Living expenses and debt retirement are categories of cash-flow requirements that are paid with after-tax dollars in almost every case. Therefore, if the objective is to pay zero taxes, all living expenses and debt retirement must be paid with either borrowed funds or not paid at all.

For example, if Bob and Laura decide to pay off their home mortgage of $81,500, that means over time they must generate, after taxes, $81,500 with which to pay that debt. There is no way they can

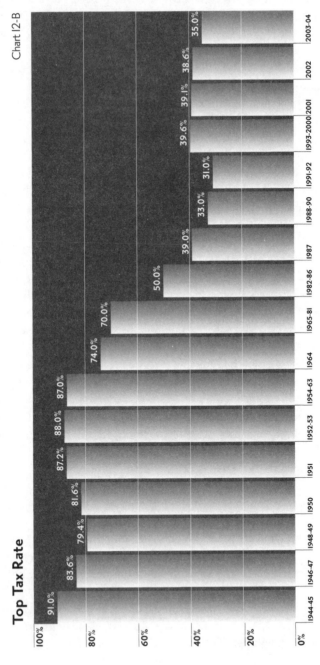

Chart 12-B

Top Tax Rate

Year	Rate
1944-45	91.0%
1946-47	83.6%
1948-49	79.4%
1950	81.6%
1951	87.2%
1952-53	88.0%
1954-63	87.0%
1964	74.0%
1965-81	70.0%
1982-86	50.0%
1987	39.0%
1988-90	33.0%
1991-92	31.0%
1993-2000	39.6%
2001	39.1%
2002	38.6%
2003-04	35.0%

pay the debt with pretax dollars. By the same token, if their objective is to have $30,000 of living expenses this year, then they must generate, after taxes, after giving, and after debt repayment, $30,000. The lower the effective tax rate, the more easily this is accomplished. The question is, how can you reduce your effective tax rate? Remember, the effective rate is far more important than the tax bracket or marginal rate.

Tax Planning Strategies

The most popular time for tax planning by taxpayers is December, with the second most popular month being April. However, both months are too late to do any serious tax planning. Once December 31 has passed, nothing can be done, other than an IRA or pension plan investment, to reduce taxes for the previous year. Most people know this and become rather panicked in the month of December, wondering how they are going to reduce their taxes. My general rule for tax planning is:

The shorter the perspective on tax planning, the higher the risk that must be taken and/or the fewer the options that are available.

I believe that most income tax planning should be done at least one year in advance with monitoring and the necessary adjustments made in the plan at least quarterly during the year. This means that the tax planning you do on December 31 would *not* be for the current year, but for the next year, so that you are always one year ahead. Tax planning is much like a funnel—at the beginning of the year, the options are many, but as you go through the year, the funnel narrows and the options become fewer. As a stream of liquid passing through the funnel rushes more rapidly near the nozzle, so the emotional intensity increases as the year goes by. The end of the year, with so few options available and so much emotion being generated, is the time when many poor tax-planning decisions are made.

All tax planning falls into four general tax planning strategies: timing, shifting, investing, and use of the tax law. You don't need to be an expert to understand these four general strategies, but you need merely to ask yourself four questions:

1. *Timing.* Can I reduce my taxes by changing the year I am to receive income or to pay deductible expenses in?

2. *Shifting.* Can I reduce my taxes by shifting my income to someone in my family who is in a lower tax bracket?

3. *Investing.* Can I reduce my taxes through the use of investments?

4. *Use of tax law.* Can I reduce my taxes through the wise use of any additional tax law provisions that I am not now using?

Timing Strategies

Timing strategies involve the timing of the recognition of income and the deduction of expenses. The general rule is that you should always push income into a future year and pull expenses into the current year. Why? Because, even if these actions do not change the tax bracket one way or the other, they do delay the payment of taxes. For example, if a taxpayer is in the 15 percent tax bracket and has the opportunity to delay $1,000 of income, it will reduce the current taxes by $150; but because that income went into the next year, it increases the taxes paid next year by $150. That may not seem to make any difference; however, the taxpayer, not the government, has had the use of $150 for one year and the time to earn interest on that $150. Previously, we saw how a little bit over a long time period can add up to a great deal through the magic of compounding.

Accelerating or pulling deductions into the current year has the same effect. For example, if a taxpayer is in the 15 percent tax bracket and pulls $1,000 of deductions from next year into this year, the tax liability goes down $150 for the current year and up $150 for the next year. As above, this strategy enables the taxpayer to control the $150 for a longer time.

In considering this strategy, the doctrine in tax law called "Constructive Receipt" must be understood. The doctrine of Constructive Receipt simply says that if you earn the income and have a right to receive it, you cannot postpone the taxes incurred on that amount by merely choosing not to receive it.

For example, a person offering professional services receives checks near the end of the year, but in an effort to avoid taxable income, he merely sticks them in a bottom drawer and does not deposit them until after December 31. This violates the doctrine of Constructive Receipt. He is attempting to use a timing strategy in reducing his income, but as a matter of fact, it is tax evasion, not tax avoidance. He must receive and report the income.

There are many legal ways to defer income, such as postponing the work that would generate the income or delaying the billing for such work so that the payment received for it is not due until the following year. Also, money invested in a savings type of account, such as a money market fund, is taxed as the interest is earned on a daily basis. Instead of leaving the money in such an account, invest it in a Treasury Bill that has a maturity date beyond the end of the year. Then the income generated by that investment is taxed in the subsequent year rather than the current year.

An employer/owner of a corporation can choose to pay bonuses after the end of the calendar year, thereby postponing the tax on that income until the next year. There are other ways to defer income, but my objective here is to challenge your thinking and your own creativity rather than to provide a tax manual.

Some of the obvious ways to pull deductions into the current year are to pay for all expenses incurred, but not yet due, prior to the end of the year—for example, interest on debt that has been incurred, medical expenses that have been incurred but not yet paid, property taxes, legal fees, state income taxes, and so on. You cannot, according to the law, prepay interest and medical expenses, but you can bring the payments up-to-date, thereby deducting them in the current year as opposed to the subsequent year. You will need to be alert for these deductions as delayed billing in December is increasingly common by professionals (they are trying to work their own timing strategy for income).

My recommendation is that you review last year's tax return and ask yourself the question for each item of income, "Could it have been deferred into the subsequent year?" And for each deduction you took, ask yourself the question, "Could I have pulled more deductions in this area from the subsequent year?" Because of their nature, timing strategies are about the only strategies that work near the end of the year. Almost all of the other strategies must be implemented earlier in the year.

Shifting Strategies

Understanding tax brackets is essential for understanding shifting strategies. The shifting strategies ask the question, "Can I shift what would be taxable income to me to a taxpaying entity in a lower tax bracket?" For example, can I shift income from my wife and me, who are in a high tax bracket, to our children, who are in a very low tax bracket, and perhaps pay no taxes at all? The assumption in using this type of strategy is that I can shift the income and either still retain control of that income or use it for an item that I would have paid for anyway.

Probably the classic example of shifting income is in the area of providing for the college education of children. Many times parents will have the opportunity to give their children over the age of thirteen income-producing assets so that the child can pay the income taxes earned on that income rather than the parent and use the income left over, after paying taxes, to pay for a college education.

For example, if the college education costs are $9,000 per year and the parents are paying that cost, they must earn the $9,000 plus the income taxes in order to have $9,000 left over to pay for the college education. If their tax bracket is 30 percent, then they must earn approximately $12,857 to have $9,000 left over with which to pay education costs. If, on the other hand, the child is in the 15 percent tax bracket, he or she can earn $10,588, pay the taxes, and still have $9,000 left over. The parents, then, have paid for the college education for that year with substantially fewer dollars than had they paid the taxes on their earnings and then funded the college education with after-tax earnings.

Recent tax law changes have brought better tax-advantaged ways of saving for education expenses than the classic shifting example mentioned in the previous paragraph. The Coverdell Education Savings Account (ESA) provides tax-free growth if the withdrawals are used to pay education expenses. Parents may invest up to $2,000 each year for each child/student. The ESA may be invested in various mutual funds. Let's say that a parent contributes $2,000 for one year only. Over time, the investments in this ESA are assumed to increase to $5,000. When the parents withdraw the $5,000 to help pay for education costs, there is no tax due! The growth is not simply tax deferred, but tax free.

If parents (or grandparents or others) want to contribute more than $2,000 per child per year, then another alternative is the 529 plan. Named after the Internal Revenue Code Section 529, the 529 plan offers tax-free growth similar to the ESA. However, a maximum of $55,000 may be contributed at once. Contributions to 529 plans are removed from the donor's estate and are no longer taxed if the withdrawals are used for education. Once again, tax-free growth! Mutual fund companies have teamed up with states to offer these plans. The 529 legal landscape has been changing regularly since their recent introduction; therefore, I would recommend working with a financial adviser who can guide you as to the best choice.

In addition, many states offer various prepaid tuition programs. Although the various options present more complexity, think of them as a blessing. When I was saving for and assisting my children with college costs, I didn't have these outstanding tax-advantaged plans available.

The shifting strategy and funding of tax-advantaged accounts typically works best within a family. The reason these strategies work best within families is that the ultimate objective is not to give away money, but to reduce taxes on income that is earned. You could, for example, give me $11,000 of income-producing assets (which, incidentally, I would gladly accept). However, you are out-of-pocket for the total gift. Your income taxes would decrease, but you gave up the assets and this would not make good economic sense. But if you put mutual funds producing $11,000 in your child's name to pay for college or in an ESA or 529 plan, your family will pay significantly lower taxes and your family retains control of the assets.

Gifting

The shifting strategy involves *gifting* to another family member income-producing assets, such as cash, real estate, stocks, bonds, closely held stock and notes, or mortgages receivable. Frequently these items are gifted in a trust form. The parents and an independent person act as trustee for the child's benefit. The only problem is that a gift literally must be made and the property legally transferred to the other person or trust. It cannot be loaned to them, nor transferred under any type of façade. A gift must actually be made, and if the gift is large enough, a gift tax may have to be paid.

Investment

The goal of every investment you make is to produce more value or more income over time. Income from investments is taxed in various ways and can, therefore, have a great impact on total taxes paid. Income investments are taxed in four ways.

Tax-exempt/tax-free

The income from some investments, such as municipal bonds, is tax-exempt by law, and as a result, this income is substantially lower than the fully taxable income earned on similar types of investments.

Roth IRAs, named after Senator William Roth, who initially proposed the legislation authorizing them, provide tax-free returns. Any contributions to a Roth IRA is after tax, but any appreciation, interest, or dividends are tax free. Inside of your Roth IRA you can invest in mutual funds, individual stocks, or certificates of deposit. Roth IRAs are excellent vehicles for retirement and long-term savings. To be eligible, you must have earned income and total adjusted gross income less than $160,000 (2004 limit) for a married filing jointly couple.

Tax-deferred

Some investments require that no tax be paid on the income earned until some time in the future. Almost all retirement plans fall into this category, whether it is an employer-sponsored plan such as a 401(k) or 403(b), or one of your own retirement plans such as a traditional IRA, SEP, or another qualified retirement plan. In addition, tax-deferred annuities from insurance companies allow you to earn a return on a tax-deferred basis.

The value of a tax-deferred investment is that compounding works for you not only on your portion of the income earned on the investment but also on the portion that would have gone to pay taxes, had they not been deferred. Additionally, when it is time to pay taxes on the investment income that has been generated, presumably the investor is retired and in a lower tax bracket and, therefore, in real dollar terms, pays less in income taxes.

These instruments are excellent ways to avoid taxes now and save for future long-term goals.

Tax-favored

Tax-favored investments are investments having special income tax allowances and provisions, again merely as a matter of law and not because of the nature of the investment. For example, most oil and gas tax investments enjoy a favored status due to the depletion allowance.

Fully Taxable

The fourth type of investment is one that is fully taxable and includes almost all interest-bearing types of investments other than those described above.

Remember that anytime there is a favorable tax consequence to an investment, there is a corresponding cost somewhere. For example, in the tax-exempt municipal bonds, the cost is that the yield is not as high as in fully taxable investments. In the case of tax-deferred investments, the cost is that the investment is not accessible—unless you pay the penalties for early withdrawals. In the area of tax-favored investments, the cost is typically in the higher risk associated with those investments.

To give you an idea of the consequences of the taxability of income and what that means in terms of your ability to accumulate, the following chart assumes a $1,000 investment per year. The tax-free investment return is 5 percent; the tax-deferred investment return is 8 percent; the fully taxable return, also at 8 percent, is assumed at a 25 percent marginal tax rate.

In reviewing chart 12-C, it is easy to see that the tax bracket you are in has a major bearing on the relative attractiveness of the investment. At the end of forty years in the tax-deferred investment, you could begin drawing an amount at 10 percent per year and would have both a return of principal and income in terms of the taxable consequence of that withdrawal. If we assume the withdrawal is 10 percent per year and that all of the withdrawal is interest and fully taxable and the remaining continues to earn 8 percent, the tax-deferred fund is still not depleted until *twenty-two years* in the future. Compare this to withdrawing the same $29,500 from the other funds, which results in total depletion of the tax-free fund after five years, of the fully taxable fund at the 25 percent tax rate in six and a half years.

As you get older, the tax-free nature of certain income may appear desirable. However, the illustration shows the value of compounding on a tax-deferred basis as compared to any other alternative. Tax-free bonds do not yield enough to offset the compounding impact on a tax-deferred basis, nor do they offset the compounding associated with fully taxable amounts for the taxpayer in the 25 percent bracket in this illustration. If you qualify for a Roth IRA, it may provide the best of both worlds by providing tax-free returns and higher potential yields than tax-exempt bonds.

Difference Between "Tax-free" & "Tax-deferred" Chart 12-C

YEAR	5% TAX-FREE	8% YIELD TAX-DEFERRED	8% YIELD 25% TAX BRACKET
1	$1,050	$1,080	$1,060
5	5,525	5,867	5,637
10	12,578	14,487	13,181
15	21,579	27,152	23,276
20	33,067	45,762	36,786
25	47,727	73,106	54,864
30	66,439	113,283	79,058
35	90,320	172,317	111,435
40	127,800	295,056	154,762
Years the fund will last if it continues to earn interest but a withdrawal of $29,500 per year is made	5.0	22.0	6.5

The primary point is that there are different types of tax-favored investments. When making an investment decision, base your decision first of all on investment considerations and, second, on tax considerations.

Use of Tax Law Provisions

The last strategy to use in tax planning is to review all the tax law provisions that allow for deductions, deferrals, credits, and the like to make sure you are using all that are applicable to your situation. These provisions are somewhat technical and fill pages of the Internal Revenue Code, so I will explain only the major categories, and then in each category, list some of the tax law provisions that might be applicable. Review these and seek advice from a professional if you think they are applicable.

Adjustments to Income

Adjustments to income are just exactly that—certain expenditures that adjust the income reported on the tax form in order to compute what is called "adjusted gross income." Adjusted gross income is an important number, because some deductions on the tax return relate to that number. The most common adjustments allowable to income are traditional IRA contributions, retirement plan contributions of self-employed individuals, alimony paid (not child support), student loan interest, moving expenses, teacher's unreimbursed expenses, and others.

Itemized Deductions

Some itemized deductions that are allowable are medical and dental expenses (when your expenses exceed a percentage of your adjusted gross income); state and local taxes, including property taxes, income taxes, and all personal property taxes; mortgage and investment interest paid; charitable contributions of either cash or property; and investment-related expenses.

I am often asked whether contributions of time are deductible, and the answer is no. If you do not receive income for the time spent, you already have received, in effect, a deduction by not having the income to report as taxable income.

The most commonly overlooked itemized deductions are:

- ❖ Expenses paid as a volunteer for charitable organizations
- ❖ Points paid on a purchase of a personal residence
- ❖ Personal property taxes

Tax Credits

In addition to deductions and adjustments to income, the tax law provides for tax credits that reduce taxes dollar for dollar, whereas adjustments and deductions do not.

The principal tax credits include the child tax credits, child and dependent care credit for expenses paid by a working couple, adoption credit, college credit, and a contribution to a retirement plan credit.

Special Provisions

In addition, the IRS has special provisions for certain situations such as the exclusion of the sale of a principal residence, exemptions for each dependent, and for many, many other situations and items.

Using the tax law provisions typically requires expert counsel, but you should review the tax return package sent to you by the government very thoroughly. The preparation of the income tax return is distasteful for most of us, and therefore we fail to pay close enough attention to all of the provisions that will help us reduce our taxes.

Special Opportunity

Ours is one of the few countries in the world that allows charitable deductions for income tax purposes. One of the principal advantages that our government allows in this area is the deduction of the full fair market value of a gift of property. For example, if you had purchased a stock for $10,000 and it had appreciated in value to $20,000, and if you sold that stock and paid the tax on it of, say, $1,500, you would have $18,500 left to give to a charitable organization. The $18,500 contribution would further reduce your taxes by (for illustration purposes) 25 percent or $4,625, so that the net cost to making the charitable contribution would be the $20,000 property less the $4,625 tax savings or $15,375.

If, on the other hand, the stock had been contributed directly to the charitable organization, there would have been a $20,000 contribution allowed, with a tax savings of $5,000, for a lower net cost to you of $15,000. The charity, in turn, could sell the property for $20,000 and have $20,000 rather than $18,500, and it would have cost the taxpayer $375 less ($5,000–$4,625) to give a charity $1,500 more ($20,000–$18,500). Obviously, this is a "win-win" situation. Chart 12-D illustrates this opportunity for taxpayers.

One important caveat in gifting appreciated property is that the appreciation amount, while not subject to regular tax, is subject to the Alternative Minimum Tax, if you fall into that category. If you suspect you may be subject to the Alternative Minimum Tax (or are gifting a substantially appreciated asset), see a tax professional for help.

Advantages of Charitable Giving

Chart 12-D

GIVE CASH	
	25% ORDINARY INCOME TAX BRACKET
Sale price	$20,000
Tax on Gain (Capital gain = 15%)	(1,500)
Given to charities	18,500
Tax on savings	$4,625
COST TO GIVER	
Stock value	$20,000
Less tax savings	(4,625)
Actual cost	$15,375

GIVE PROPERTY	
	25% ORDINARY INCOME TAX BRACKET
Given to charities	$20,000
Tax savings	(5,000)
Actual cost	15,000
Savings to donor	375
Increased gift to charity	$1,500

Action to Be Taken

As a taxpayer you can take three steps. First, determine the projected tax liability for the following year as early in the year as possible; second, plan to reduce that liability through the many items discussed here; and third, set the withholding amount and tax estimate amount at the accurate projected liability amount.

To avoid a penalty, most taxpayers have to pay in estimated tax or withholding at least equal to their last year's tax liability or 90 percent of his current year's liability, whichever one is less. (High-income taxpayers with joint incomes over $150,000 must pay in at least 110 percent of the past year's tax liability to avoid a penalty.) As I said earlier, to receive a tax refund is a sign of poor planning. I recommend that you determine your projected tax liability simply by taking last year's tax return and projecting to the best of your knowledge what the numbers will be this year. Use the chart on page 179.

After doing this, determine the withholding amounts paid year to date, compared to what will be paid in if the withholdings stay at the same level. If needed, you can adjust the withholding to the newly determined amount. In the tax year of 2002, nearly 100,000,000 tax-payers received refunds (three out of every four returns). The average refund was nearly $2,000.[1] In effect, what they had done was make an interest-free loan to the government for $2,000 for one year.

In Bob and Laura's case, they determined that by reducing with-holdings to the rate that coincides with what they would actually receive, they could generate an additional $2,500 of cash flow this year. Additionally, they need to make a decision about whether or not to contribute to a traditional IRA for both of them. Because they do not have the excess cash flow to do so, they would have to decide whether that money should come out of their savings account or they could use their improved cash flow from adjusting tax withholdings. They probably should make the contribution to the IRA, but we will discuss investments further for them in the next chapter.

Conclusion

Tax planning must be integrated with all other types of planning. However, tax planning should not be the "tail that wags the dog"; it should rather remain the tail. Investment planning requires, first of all, that you make a good investment and then consider the tax con-sequences, rather than make the investment for tax consequences. That goes for charitable contributions, estate planning, and any other type of financial decision.

Tax planning is very important, but it is not a panacea for cash-flow problems. Every decision that causes a reduction in taxes has a corresponding cost associated with it. Therefore, reducing taxes may increase cash flow in the short term, but there is a cost associated with it, and that must be considered. Just remember, there is no "free lunch," especially in the cafeteria of tax reductions.

Tax planning can and will change as Congress changes tax laws, as the IRS decides how to administer the law, and as the courts inter-pret the law. The principles contained in this chapter almost certainly *won't* change as long as we have a graduated income tax system, but the specific application may vary as laws are changed.

Endnote:

1. "Big Refund? Big Tax Bill?" article published in 2002 by the Internal Revenue Service on its website at www.irs.gov.

Income Tax Analysis

Chart 12-E

	LAST YEAR	ESTIMATED THIS YEAR
INCOME:		
Salary		
Interest & dividends		
Net business income (Schedule C)		
State tax refund		
Capital gains income (Schedule D)		
Rental and S-Corp. income (Schedule E)		
Other		
GROSS INCOME		
LESS ADJUSTMENT TO INCOME:		
Traditional IRA		
Other (moving, student loan, interest)		
ADJUSTED GROSS INCOME (A.G.I.)		
LESS ITEMIZED DEDUCTIONS:		
Medical expenses over 7.5% of A.G.I.		
Taxes		
Interest		
Contributions		
Miscellaneous over 2% of A.G.I.		
TOTAL DEDUCTIONS		
LESS EXEMPTIONS		
TAXABLE INCOME		
FEDERAL INCOME TAX		
PLUS OTHER TAXES:		
Self-employment tax		
Other		
LESS CREDITS:		
Children		
Child care		
College		
Other		
TOTAL FEDERAL TAX		
TOTAL STATE TAX		
TOTAL TAX		
MARGINAL TAX RATE		
EFFECTIVE TAX RATE		

INVESTMENT PLANNING

People tend to think that because I am a Christian financial planner I am against acquiring material possessions or accumulations. Once Judy and I were with a woman who showed us a very large diamond she was wearing. She quickly explained that the diamond was an "investment." I smiled and wondered to myself how high the price of diamonds would have to go before that diamond would be sold. My opinion was that the diamond would not be taken off the woman's finger at any price.

An investment is something that is purchased with the intent to resell at a higher price. Therefore, diamonds, expensive cars, vacation homes, antiques, and even your home never qualify as investments. They are purchases that may go up in value and consequently prove to be a wise purchase, but they are not investments. Many people delude themselves into calling a purchase an investment in order to justify its purchase, but it is never an investment unless it was purchased to preserve or increase its value, and, ultimately, to resell it at a higher price than what was paid for it, or for it to provide some amount of economic return or yield.

It is *critical* that you understand the difference between an investment and a purchase, because different criteria are used to evaluate each one. In this chapter, we will only be dealing with investments—items purchased solely either to generate a current yield to the investor or to grow in value, or to do both. If they are not accomplishing the intended objective, then they should be sold immediately.

Most Common Investment Mistakes

From my own experience and from working with many others, I have heard about many so-called "good deals." Obviously, not all of these deals are good deals. But on the front end, they always seem to be. Good deals only become bad deals over time, and I have learned something: *There will be as good a deal tomorrow as there is today.* Therefore, I never have to respond to the "good deal" that is presented to me today regardless of how good it is, because my experience has shown that I will have another one tomorrow and another one the next day, and another one the next day, and another one the next day.

In evaluating investments, many fall into the "binary trap." The binary trap centers on the question, should I do this or not? It only gives me two alternatives—yes or no—and if the deal is a good deal I most certainly should say yes to it. However, to avoid the binary trap, ask the question, if this is a good deal, is it the best use of my available funds? When I evaluate an investment this way, I immediately open up many more alternatives to investing than just the one presented.

Unless there is a long-term investment strategy in place, you will always be subject to falling into the binary trap. The best investment for any investor depends upon one's personal long-term goals and the strategy to accomplish those goals. Then any potential investment is evaluated as part of your investment strategy, instead of assuming that every good investment is for everyone.

Rather than looking at specific investments (a major topic that needs to be covered in a separate book), I feel it is more important for you to develop and to understand your strategy. Then individual investments, as they come along, can be evaluated in light of your strategy rather than the reverse—setting your strategy on the basis of the investments you have made.

From an investment standpoint, we have basically three time periods of life. The time period when we are working to meet long-term goals I simply call *the accumulation phase*. In this phase of life we are accumulating not only material possessions but also investments for the purpose of accomplishing our long-term goals of financial independence or starting our own business.

Once the long-term goals have been met, and we have accumulated enough by that definition, we enter the second phase of investing—*the preservation phase*. In the preservation phase we want to preserve the assets we have accumulated from uncertainties, such as inflation, deflation, stock market declines, longevity, and changing interest rates.

Financial Time Periods of Life

Figure 13.1

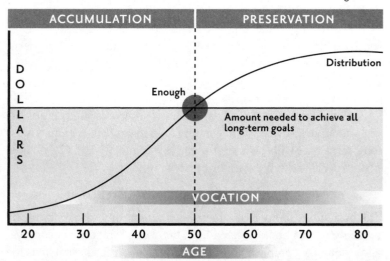

Figure 13.1 illustrates these two time periods of an investor's life. Basically, from age twenty to approximately age fifty, we are accumulating material possessions, paying off debt, and raising our families. The major accumulation of investments begins to take place between the ages of forty and fifty, and at some point during this time period we may cross the line of having accumulated enough to meet our

long-term goals. However, almost no one stops accumulating at this point for one very good reason—the uncertainty of our economic environment. Some time around the age of sixty, we shift to a preservation mode where we are attempting to preserve our assets in light of the risks.

Then at some point between sixty and eighty, we enter the *distribution phase*. The distribution phase of investment planning can be either immediate, in the event of death, or planned to take place over a long term. We will discuss the distribution phase of life in chapter 14 on estate planning.

Obviously, the graph will be different for different people. Some of us achieve our long-term goals very early; others of us never achieve our long-term goals. The point is to understand where you are and what that means for your investment strategy. You need to know if you are in an accumulation strategy or a preservation strategy because the investment techniques and the type of investment to be considered are different for each strategy.

It is also important to know what level of accumulation (represented by the line on the graph) is needed to meet the long-term goals. That number and that line define how much is enough. When you go beyond that line, you have to answer the question, why am I continuing to accumulate?

The two key questions to ask yourself when considering investing and an investment strategy are: (1) Why am I investing? (What long-term goal will this investment help to meet?) and (2) What is my purpose—accumulation or preservation?

Accumulation Investment Strategy

The basic philosophy that I have been attempting to communicate throughout this book is that a little bit over a long time period will allow you to accomplish your long-term goals. The alternative is the attempt to get rich quick and live with the high risk of losing it all. Most persons invest by responding rather than planning. I hope by this point you are convinced that planning your investments, rather than responding to the alternatives presented to you, is a far more secure path to achieving your long-term financial goals.

First of all, the accumulation strategy revolves around having a cash-flow margin and then making a decision regarding the use of

this margin. You say, "The best use of this margin is _____."
The "best" will depend on four things—your personal goals, the commitments you already have, your personal priorities, and all the other alternatives for spending this margin.

I have a recommendation for the sequential use of your cash-flow margin, and I call it the Sequential Accumulation Strategy. With this investment strategy, you use the first dollar of cash-flow margin to accomplish step 1. After you complete step 1, then move to step 2, and so on. The following is a description of each step.

Step 1: Eliminate all credit card and consumer debt. This, as explained earlier, provides an immediate "investment return" of 12 percent to 21 percent. Not having to pay that interest cost each year is, in effect, the same as achieving the same rate of return on any monies invested by you. Therefore, it is the surest and highest form of investment return you can make.

Step 2: Set aside one month's living expenses in the checking account. This is in addition to the current month's living expenses that are in the checking account, so at the beginning of any one month there would be two month's living expenses already deposited in the checking account. This "investment" is for flexibility.

Step 3: Invest between three and six months' living expenses in an interest-bearing money market fund account. This becomes the emergency fund and, in effect, your own bank. As you need money to make a major purchase or have an unexpected major expense or see an opportunity to save through purchasing now instead of later, you can borrow from yourself out of this account rather than from a lending institution. If you tap into this account for an emergency, replace it as soon as possible. Steps 2 and 3 provide you with flexibility so that you will be prepared for emergencies that may deplete your resources or cause further debt.

Step 4: Save in an interest-bearing account for major purchases. This is the planned purchase of major items such as automobiles, furniture, and even the down payment on a home.

Steps 1 through 4 should be done in sequence rather than all at once. In other words, you do not go to step 3 until you have accomplished step 2. By doing so, you eliminate the need to make a decision whenever an investment alternative comes to you. If you have not already accomplished steps 1 through 4, you let the option go by.

This takes discipline, but it is the right thing to do.

Step 5: Accumulate to meet long-term goals. The long-term goals of financial independence, college education, giving beyond the tithe, owning your own business, paying off mortgage debt, and major lifestyle changes, as depicted in your Financial Planning Diagram, are now funded through various investment alternatives. These investment alternatives provide a greater potential return to meet your long-term goals and involve more risk. However, you can likely accept more risk if you have a cash-flow margin, have an emergency savings reserve, and have reduced short-term debt.

Sequential Accumulation Strategy

Figure 13.2

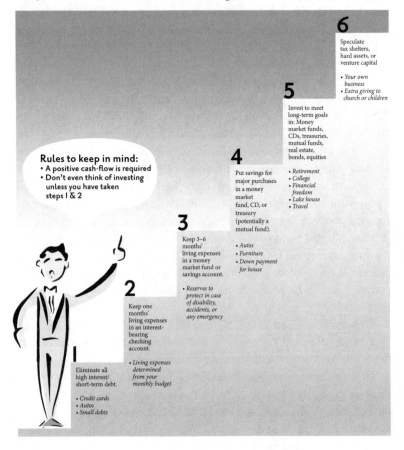

6
Speculate
tax shelters,
hard assets, or
venture capital

• *Your own
business*
• *Extra giving to
church or children*

5
Invest to meet
long-term goals
in: Money
market funds,
CDs, treasuries,
mutual funds,
real estate,
bonds, equities

Rules to keep in mind:
• A positive cash-flow is required
• Don't even think of investing
unless you have taken
steps 1 & 2

4
Put savings for
major purchases
in a money
market
fund, CD, or
treasury
(potentially a
mutual fund).

• *Retirement*
• *College*
• *Financial
freedom*
• *Lake house*
• *Travel*

3
Keep 3–6
months'
living expenses
in a money
market fund or
savings account.

• *Autos*
• *Furniture*
• *Down payment
for house*

2
Keep one
months'
living expenses
in an interest-
bearing
checking
account.

• *Reserves to
protect in case
of disability,
accidents, or
any emergency*

1
Eliminate all
high interest/
short-term debt.

• *Living expenses
determined
from your
monthly budget*

• *Credit cards*
• *Autos*
• *Small debts*

Step 6: Use investment dollars to speculate in higher ⌐
ments. At this point, by definition, every short-term and ⌐
goal has already been met. I have seen very few people ev ⌐
this step of investing, and coincidentally, those who have do ⌐
to speculate because they don't want to risk the loss. They prえ ⌐o
adopt what I have called the "preservation investment strategy."

Let me repeat that *the sequential investment strategy is totally de-pendent upon having a positive cash-flow margin.* As you have a positive cash flow, the first priority use of that cash is step 1, and so forth in sequence. This sequence obviously represents my opinion about what the priorities should be; your priorities may be different. For example, step 4 may be a higher priority for you than my step 3, and that is perfectly acceptable. The important point is to prayerfully set your priorities and to have a strategy for meeting them.

You may even decide to do your investing concurrently rather than sequentially. I believe steps 1 and 2 must be met first, but then steps 3, 4, and 5 could be met concurrently with the cash-flow margin for the year allocated in the following way:

To step 3—40%		30%		?%	
To step 4—40%	or	60%	or	?%	
To step 5—20%		10%		?%	
Total 100%		100%		100%	

Do not forget your strategy and become involved in premature investing and speculation.

Investment Vehicles and Techniques Versus Investments

In addition to understanding specific investment products, such as stocks, bonds, T-bills, gold, silver, land, mutual funds, and apartments, you need to know the investment vehicles and techniques for investing in these specific products. Don't confuse the investment vehicle with the investment. For example, some people ask me, "What do IRAs yield?" Well, the question doesn't make sense. An IRA is a *vehicle* allowed by the government. You get to choose what investment products to put in that vehicle. You could invest in individual stocks, a CD, or mutual funds. So, the answer to the question about what do IRAs yield is, "It depends." It depends on what the ıRA (investment vehicle) has invested in (the actual investments). Other vehicles include 401(k)s, variable annuities, ESAs, 529 plans, cash balance pension plans, and many more.

Dollar cost averaging, which is a strategy of committing a fixed amount of money per month to a particular investment resulting in a low per-unit cost, is a *technique* of investing. I think it is a good technique to establish the discipline of regular investing and eliminate the emotions of investing. The ultimate result of this technique depends on the actual investment's performance and when the sale occurs. Market timing is a *technique* of buying and selling stocks or mutual funds according to a mathematical formula; one hopes that over time they can be successful in selling near the top of the market and buying near the bottom of the market.

Each of these vehicles and techniques uses one of the specific investment products to accomplish its objective. The vehicles and techniques require a great deal of experience and expertise to be effective and should be utilized by the investor only with assistance of a qualified financial adviser (see www.cfpn.org for financial advisers in the Christian Financial Professionals Network). The financial adviser can help you know whether the vehicle or technique fits your situation and then how to pair the best investments with the best vehicles and techniques. These vehicles and techniques can be used either during the accumulation or the preservation phase of investing.

Specific Investments

For those who are still accumulating, I recommend three primary types of investments:

1. Money Market Instruments

These investment products are liquid, provide competitive interest rates, and have very little risk of loss of principal except in an inflationary time. Specifically, these investments would include certificates of deposit, treasury bills, savings accounts, and money market funds.

The advantage of a money market fund type of investment or any other short-term, interest-bearing investment is that you have professional money managers managing your investment in order to achieve the highest return at the lowest risk while maintaining total liquidity of the investment. Therefore, you don't have to guess about whether interest rates are going up or down, and you always have the opportunity to move the money out of the money market fund if a better alternative investment comes along.

2. Mutual Funds

A mutual fund is, in effect, a pooled fund of money from many investors that is entrusted to a professional investment manager. There are almost as many types of mutual funds as there are investment objectives. The three main types are long-term growth funds that invest primarily in the stock market, income funds that invest in bonds and other high-yielding investments, and a combination of income and growth funds that attempt to achieve both objectives.

The advantage of using mutual funds for accumulation is that you achieve professional management, diversification in your investments, liquidity of your money, and many alternatives to fit your risk level.

3. Real Estate Investments

For many investors, Real Estate Investment Trusts (REITs) are becoming the preferred method to invest in real estate. Unlike other forms of real estate, shares in REITs are priced daily and traded like stocks. REITs typically specialize in their investment selection and focus on one type of real estate such as apartments, retail centers, shopping malls, hotels, office buildings, etc. Because it is extremely hard to value REITs, the individual investor is often better served by investing in a fund that purchases shares of different REITs. In doing this investors can enjoy a great amount of diversification by adding an asset class to their investment portfolios that should reduce the volatility of their overall holdings.

Preservation Investment Strategy

The perfect investment is one that is totally liquid, with no risk, yielding a high percentage of return, and growing at a rate greater than the inflation rate. I have yet to see the perfect investment because there are always trade-offs. An investment that is liquid typically does not grow in value—for example, a savings account. On the other hand, one that is growing in value, such as real estate, probably bears some risk, may not have a yield associated with it, and certainly is not liquid.

A good investment strategy for *the entire investment portfolio* accomplishes four specifically quantified universal investment objectives: (1) maximize liquidity, (2) maximize growth, (3) maximize yield, and (4) minimize risk. Of these four objectives, investors will have different priorities that are dependent upon a variety of things.

Age. A younger person needs less liquidity, takes more risk, needs more growth, and can accept less yield.

Temperament. Some people can stand no risk and want all of their money invested in certificates of deposit. Others have the philosophy "Try to hit a home run—even if we strike out."

Tax situation. Those in the higher tax brackets are more typically concerned with growth than they are yield because the tax on the growth is deferred, whereas yield is typically taxed in the current higher income tax brackets.

Other financial commitments. A debt may need to be repaid in the near future or lifestyle commitments for the near future may require more liquidity than at other times.

Certainty of future cash flow. Some people have a certainty of future cash flow through pension plans, other retirement plans, or Social Security, and the yield factor is less important for them than the growth factor. Others may have no retirement income, and therefore the yield factor is far more important to them.

The point is that each of these four universal investment objectives can be quantified, dependent upon your age, temperament, tax situation, personal philosophy, perception, and goals. Then an investment portfolio can be designed that is measurable in terms of its ability to accomplish the objectives that have been set.

Types of Risk

Once the investment portfolio has been designed and its ability to meet the universal investment objectives measured, an evaluation of the "risk" in the portfolio needs to be done. It used to be simple to define risk as merely the loss of principal. Money stored or hidden stood the risk of thieves and erosion, whereas money invested in a bank stood the risk of bank failures. However, for the most part, the risk was well-known and could be planned for. Once an investment portfolio becomes sizeable and once we introduce a worldwide and a very uncertain economic situation, the risks become far more complex and more difficult to plan for. For example:

1. *A business risk.* Some investments, such as a real estate project or a specific stock, are dependent upon the successful running of a business in order for the principal to remain intact.

2. *A financial risk.* Some investments will retain their relative value in times of monetary collapse or total economic or political upheaval, whereas others won't. For example, during a monetary collapse, real estate and gold may retain their relative value, whereas cash or stocks probably will not. Many investments, therefore, bear some financial risk.

3. *Market risks.* No one has total control of the market; rather we are subject to whatever market we happen to be investing in, whether it is the real estate market or the stock market or the bond market. Any investment that is a part of a larger market bears a risk that is basically uncontrollable by any one individual.

4. *Interest rate risk.* Many investments will provide a current interest rate, but if that interest rate is fixed and interest rates for similar types of investments go up, you have borne an interest rate risk.

5. *Purchasing power risk.* Investments in cash-type investments, such as certificates of deposit, money market funds, savings accounts, treasury bills, among other instruments, experience a loss in purchasing power during times of inflation, whereas in times of deflation, they experience an increase in purchasing power.

6. *Tax risk.* Many investments, such as tax shelters, have a risk of future assessments associated with them because the IRS may change the law or their interpretation of the law. An investment in cash probably bears no tax risk, whereas an investment in an opal mine in Brazil, yielding a large tax write-off, might bear a substantial tax risk.

7. *Legal risks.* Certain investments may have a risk of lawsuits associated with them. For example, if you are investing in rental real estate, you certainly bear the risk of a lawsuit if someone is injured on your property.

There are three ways to reduce the risk taken in any one investment or on the whole investment portfolio. First of all, become personally knowledgeable about investments and the risk you are taking before entering into an investment. Second, use experts, since no one can be an expert in everything. However, the burden of taking the risk is always on the investor rather than on the advisor. Third, do not attempt to guess the future, but rather diversify your investments so that some will be worth more over time if others will be worth less over time, depending on changing economic situations. If all investments have been properly diversified, the overall impact is that the investment portfolio has been preserved in total relative value.

Remember this *key point* because your strategy is a preservation strategy rather than an accumulation strategy. All of the accumulating has already been done. Now you are preserving the assets or investments relative to all of the risks and relative to the goals and objectives that you have. If you knew with certainty the future, you would not diversify; you would "put all of your eggs in one basket." The best way to prepare for the future and to preserve the investments that you have accumulated is to diversify, diversify, and diversify again.

There is absolutely no way to avoid all risks, and quite frankly, the number one objective is not necessarily to avoid all the risks. It is to try to use, grow, and give God's provision to the best of my human ability under His guidance. *Human* is an important word. We cannot see the future. We do not have all resources at our fingertips, but God does. God owns all of my investments and your investments and is in total control of the situation. If I am counting on having a risk-free investment portfolio to give me peace of mind, I will never accomplish it. The Bible has much to say about investments—more about attitude toward handling investments than about how to make investments.

Biblical Principles of Investing

1. *Do not presume upon the future.* "Now listen, you who say, 'Today or tomorrow we will go to this or that city, spend a year there, carry on business and make money.' Why, you do not even know what will happen tomorrow. What is your life? You are a mist that appears for a little while and then vanishes. Instead, you ought

to say, 'If it is the Lord's will, we will live and do this or that'" (James 4:13–15 NIV).

2. *Avoid speculation and hasty investment decisions, especially those motivated by greed or fear.* "Dishonest money dwindles away, but he who gathers money little by little makes it grow" (Proverbs 13:11 NIV). "A faithful man will be richly blessed, but one eager to get rich will not go unpunished" (Proverbs 28:20 NIV). "A stingy man is eager to get rich and is unaware that poverty awaits him" (Proverbs 28:22 NIV).

3. *Never cosign.* "He who puts up security for another will surely suffer, but whoever refuses to strike hands in pledge is safe" (Proverbs 11:15 NIV). "A man lacking in judgment strikes hands in pledge and puts up security for his neighbor" (Proverbs 17:18 NIV). "Do not be a man who strikes hands in pledge or puts up security for debts; if you lack the means to pay, your very bed will be snatched from under you" (Proverbs 22:26–27 NIV).

4. *Evaluate the risk of an investment.* "Suppose one of you wants to build a tower. Will he not first sit down and estimate the cost to see if he has enough money to complete it?" (Luke 14:28 NIV). In other words, is the risk that you are taking worth it? Why are you taking the risk? If the risk does happen, can you afford to lose your investment dollar? Will that change anything for you financially?

5. *Avoid investments that cause anxiety.* "My heart is not proud, O LORD, my eyes are not haughty; I do not concern myself with great matters or things too wonderful for me" (Psalm 131:1 NIV). "So do not worry, saying, 'What shall we eat?' or 'What shall we drink?' or 'What shall we wear?'" (Matthew 6:31 NIV).

6. *Be in unity with your spouse.* Throughout Scripture we are admonished to counsel together and to have a unity in the husband/wife relationship. Often God uses our mates to bring us back to reality. Don't be so foolish or proud and do not take advantage of the partner God has given you.

7. *Avoid high leverage situations.* "The rich rule over the poor, and the borrower is servant to the lender" (Proverbs 22:7 NIV).

8. *Avoid deceit.* "The wicked man earns deceptive wages, but he who sows righteousness reaps a sure reward" (Proverbs 11:18 NIV).

9. *Tithe from your investment gains.* Many investors believe that it makes good sense to keep the investment dollars and their increases to make additional investments. Usually the rationale is that they will receive greater tax advantages and be able to multiply these resources even more for the Lord. This rationale is unscriptural because God expects a portion of the increase. "Honor the LORD with your wealth, with the firstfruits of all your crops; then your barns will be filled to overflowing, and your vats will brim over with new wine" (Proverbs 3:9–10 NIV). Although it is practically difficult to tithe on the change in value during a month or a quarter, I do recommend tithing when you sell an investment holding (outside of a retirement account) and you know the amount of your realized gain.

To put off giving under the assumption that the investment will earn more and then you will have more to give is a great danger. This assumption implies that God is *incapable* of using His money today for a greater eternal impact than what I can do by investing. Let's say you have an investment, such as a mutual fund, where dividends are reinvested. When you pay taxes on your dividend annually, give your tithe on the increase then also. If you don't have the cash to give God His portion, withdraw some principal and pay it.

General Rules in Selection of Investments

We have discussed common investment mistakes, strategies, tools and techniques, the four investment criteria, risks, diversification, and biblical principles. In many ways all investment planning boils down to some very commonsense general rules.

1. *Always maintain a long-term perspective.* The longer the perspective, the better the decision is apt to be today.

2. *Remember that you can't be an expert on everything.* Be willing to trust others and avoid the pitfall of pride.

3. *High risk to one person is conservative to another.* If a person understands the stock market, stock investments may seem conservative. Another may understand nothing about the stock market, and all stock investments appear to be high risks. An oil and gas investment may be conservative to an oil and gas expert; to the

uninitiated in this type of investment, it is almost always a high-risk venture.

4. *The personal time required to manage an investment must be considered as a cost.* Many investments, such as stock portfolios, rental property, and venture capital, require personal time to ensure that they work out as they are planned. This is a very real cost to the investment, and the benefit, in relation to the cost, must be measured.

5. *Always invest from a strategy.* To do otherwise will always put you in the position of being a responder to investment alternatives as they come along. Knowing what your strategy is and the steps to accomplish this strategy will eliminate almost all investment alternatives that are proposed. Hearing about a "good deal" does not necessarily make it a good deal for you.

6. *Keep it simple.* My general rule is that if you can't explain it to your spouse, then you don't understand it, and you shouldn't do it. If an investment becomes burdensome and seemingly complex, you are probably in an area of investing that you should not be in.

7. *There is no "free lunch."* There is a definite risk/reward relationship—the higher the return you expect, the higher the risk you take. With no exception, a high return will exact a high cost.

8. *Diversify, diversify, and diversify.* Never "put all your eggs in one basket." This is the time-tested rule of investing.

Figure 13.3 illustrates how diversification of a total investment portfolio can work to reduce overall risk and increase overall return. Note, however, that not all investments go up in value all the time. It takes a very mature attitude to diversify.

The summary of what I have said in this chapter is that very few people should be involved in the high-stakes investment game because almost no one has reached the level of step 6 of the sequential investment strategy. By following the sequential investment strategy you will, by the time of your need, have accomplished almost all of your long-term goals and objectives.

Investing is not difficult, but it certainly can be confusing if you don't keep your priorities straight.

Results of Diversification

Figure 13.3

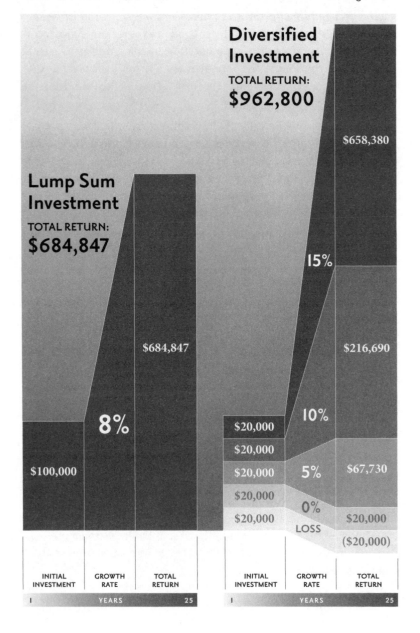

Diversified Investment
TOTAL RETURN:
$962,800

$658,380

Lump Sum Investment
TOTAL RETURN:
$684,847

$684,847

8%

$100,000

15%

$216,690

10%

$20,000
$20,000
$20,000
$20,000
$20,000

5%

$67,730

0%
LOSS

$20,000

($20,000)

INITIAL INVESTMENT	GROWTH RATE	TOTAL RETURN

| I | YEARS | 25 |

INITIAL INVESTMENT	GROWTH RATE	TOTAL RETURN

| I | YEARS | 25 |

14

STEWARDSHIP
AFTER DEATH

"Money is only useful when you get rid of it.
It is like the odd card in 'Old Maid';
the player who is finally left with it has lost."
EVELYN WAUGH

"When the heart is converted the wallet will be inverted."
ANONYMOUS

"The greatest use of life is to spend it for
something that will outlast it."
WILLIAM JAMES

You may have heard about the family who was gathered in the attorney's office eagerly awaiting the reading of the last will and testament of a recently departed family member. It did not take the attorney long to read the very simple will, which merely stated, "Being of sound mind, I spent it all." I have seen bumper stickers in a similar vein, especially near retirement communities, which say, "We're spending our kids' inheritance."

The assumption underlying both quotations is that you can know exactly when and under what circumstances you are going to die. If that is the case, you could plan to have the last penny spent at the moment of death. Unfortunately, the most frequent comment you hear is that "poor John didn't plan on dying so soon," even though "it is appointed for men to die once, but after this the judgment" (Hebrews 9:27). Everyone will die; yet very few plan on "dying so soon."

Another reality is found in 1 Timothy 6:7: "For we brought

nothing into this world, and it is certain that we can carry nothing out." To paraphrase that verse, "You never see a hearse pulling a U-Haul." John D. Rockefeller's accountant was asked one time, "Can you tell me how much Rockefeller left?" and the accountant said, "Absolutely, to the penny. Everything."

Our perspective on estate planning is based on these realities. We will all die; we will take nothing with us; and we will probably die at a time other than when we would like. These realities create many practical planning problems.

Problems Associated with Death

The most significant problem associated with death is described in Romans 6:23: "For the wages of sin is death, but the gift of God is eternal life in Christ Jesus our Lord." The person who dies without having accepted the gift of Jesus Christ as payment for his or her own sin will be eternally separated from God.

Financial problems are nonexistent in eternity. My prayer is that if any of you reading these words has never accepted the free gift of God's Son as payment for your sins, you would do so and make the most important estate planning step you can ever take. A simple prayer lays the foundation for this estate: "Father, I acknowledge my separation from You, and based upon the death of the Lord Jesus Christ as payment for my sins, I accept the free gift of salvation. Thank You for saving me."

Prior to April of 1974, my life's philosophy could have been summed up by another bumper sticker that you may have seen: "He who dies with the most toys wins." Obviously, that is a delusion, because the only one who wins when he dies is the one who has the guarantee of eternal life.

The second problem associated with death is really a set of problems relating to your finances. *Unless you plan the distribution of your estate, the government will.* Your spouse, relatives, or friends are not allowed to plan that distribution—only the owner of assets can plan the distribution through a will. Very rarely does the government have the same objectives for your estate as you do. Additionally, if proper planning has not been done, the final expenses can siphon off up to 70 percent of an estate. These expenses are for probating the will, estate taxes, inheritance taxes, attorney's fees, accountant's fees, and funeral expenses.

Another financial problem that happens frequently because of poor planning is an estate without enough liquidity to meet the final expenses. Therefore, assets must be sold at depressed values just to generate the cash needed to pay these expenses.

Parents with young children rarely plan to die; yet if they do so without proper planning, the state will determine the guardians for those surviving children. Many times, children also have special needs that call for planning if the parents are not going to be around to handle those needs.

Another problem that is associated with death, or as the life insurance industry puts it, "premature death," is that survivors usually experience handling the details of an estate only once. Consequently, there are few experts and fewer yet who can be explicitly trusted to do things exactly as you would have them do. Therefore, there is a problem of making sure that the administration of the estate is handled as you would have it handled.

Being a good steward after death requires sound planning in two areas while you are alive: *life insurance* and *estate planning*. In this chapter I will give you some general guidelines in both areas. However, since this is a very complex area and each individual situation is unique, I recommend you seek wise counsel before taking specific implementation steps. This counsel may require input from professionals such as a tax attorney, CPA, life insurance agent, bank trust officer, and financial planner. I simply want to get you started in the process.

Life Insurance Planning

Why Insurance?

The basic purpose of insurance is to transfer the risk that one is not willing to take (or is unable to take) to someone (or a company) willing to take the risk in return for compensation. In the case of life insurance, the objective is, first, to protect the family income and net worth growth in the event of the death of the breadwinner, and second, to provide protection to maintain the estate in order that it might pass on to heirs, allowing the continuation of capital from one generation to the other. (Using our Financial Planning Diagram, life insurance could be depicted by putting an umbrella over the "Growth in Net Worth" box as illustrated in Figure 14.1.) Thus the risk of loss of income or the erosion of the estate through estate taxes is passed to the insurance company. The same idea applies to the protection of houses, automobiles, and other property. Few individuals could afford to replace a house in the event of loss, so they purchase insurance for it.

The Role of Insurance

Figure 14.1

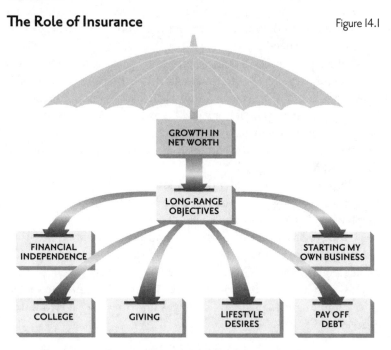

The key theme expounded in insurance sales is "protection." While this is certainly the purpose of insurance, emphasizing it also unfortunately induces an attitude of fear. Most insurance is purchased on an emotional rather than a factual basis. This attitude then leads to attempts to provide enough insurance to protect against any unknown. For the Christian, this often leads to a shifting of trust from God to insurance and to an imbalance between amounts being provided and amounts one can afford.

The perspective on insurance changes somewhat if the word *provision* is used instead of protection. God's purpose for the breadwinner, according to 1 Timothy 5:8, is to provide for the family.

Under the biblical system, when the father died, the oldest son took the breadwinner's responsibility. If a man had no son, then his brother undertook the care of the family through the laws God had established for widows and orphans (Deuteronomy 14:28–29; James 2:27). Ideally, these caring functions today would be provided by the body of Christ, the church. Unfortunately, they usually are not, so a vital part of family financial planning today is for continued provision through the use of life insurance.

You may say that purchasing insurance shows a lack of trust in God to provide. Rather, this is the sound-mind principle being put to use. If you did not purchase insurance and you are married with children, it is possible that your spouse would have to go on welfare (becoming dependent on the government) should you die prematurely. As a result, your family's spiritual and physical needs could go unmet. Insurance, on the other hand, would give your family the opportunity to continue to live in a proper environment. Insurance is not a lack of trust in God's provision; it may be a form of His provision when wisely secured. Rather insurance is acknowledgment of the certainty of death. It is consistent with the whole counsel of Scripture.

How Much Do You Need?

You can determine how much you need through the Insurance Needs Analysis Chart (chart 14-A) by first determining the insurance necessary to meet income goals and then adding to it the amount needed for long-term liquidity needs such as major expenses and estate taxes in order to facilitate the transfer of your assets from one generation to the next without tax erosion.

Insurance Needs Analysis   Chart 14-A

Income Goals for the Family	
Living expenses [1]	
Taxes	
Giving	
TOTAL INCOME NEEDED A	
Sources of income [2]	
Social Security	

Pension or retirement plans	
Annuities or trusts	
Investment income[3]	
Spouse working	
Other	
TOTAL INCOME AVAILABLE **B**	
Additional income needed (per year) [4] $B - A = C$	
Insurance Required to Provide Income [5] (Additional income needed x 10) (current need) $C \times 10 = D$	
Additional funds needed for:	
Funeral costs	
Debt repayment (current need)	
Estate tax and settlement expense (long-term need)	
Education costs (current need)	
Major purchases	
TOTAL ADDITIONAL FUNDS NEEDED **E**	
Insurance Needed [6] $E + D = F$	
Assets available for sale:	
Real estate	
Stocks, bonds	
Savings available (to meet needs listed above) [7]	
TOTAL FROM SALE OF ASSETS **G**	
Total Insurance Needed [8] $F - G = H$	
INSURANCE AVAILABLE NOW	
ADDITIONAL INSURANCE NEEDED	

NOTES

(1) Use 80% of present annual living expense.

(2) Income anticipated on a regular basis.

(3) Income from investments not liquidated.

(4) The Total Income Needed Less the Total Income Available (B – A = C).

(5) This assumes the life insurance proceeds could be invested at 10% and provide the needed amounts. The investment percentage may be contingent on economic conditions or investment knowledge. The multiplication factor is 1 divided by the percentage return on insurance proceeds.

Example: 10% = 1/.10 = 10; 8% = 1/.08 = 12.5; 12% = 1/.12 = 8.33

(6) Insurance needed is the sum of insurance to provide income (D) plus additional funds needed (E).

(7) Savings available would be only that part of savings that could be applied to meet the needs listed above. It would not include the savings needed to meet family living goals.

(8) Total insurance needed is the insurance needed less the amount available from the sale of assets (F − G = H).

Note: No adjustment has been made in these calculations for inflation. If you feel that you can earn 10% but that will be eroded by 3–4% inflation, then you should use 6–7% in step 5 and not 10%. This will increase the amount of insurance needed. You can use any investment or inflation assumption you would like.

How Long Do You Need It?

A key distinction in the Insurance Needs Analysis is the need for current provision and long-term provision. A clear delineation can help you decide between term insurance and a more permanent product.

Typically, when you are young and in the accumulation stage, and having a growing family and a lot of "current" needs (debt, education, and living expenses), you have a large need for insurance but usually limited funds with which to buy the insurance. This usually requires a purchase of term insurance.

Some consumer groups claim that buying term is always the only way to go. However, the idea of buying term and "investing the difference" is based on a short-term perspective. Although it may be sufficient to meet current needs and is much less expensive than whole life, it does get more expensive over time.

In addition, there are two good reasons to have insurance for a long-term need. First, you may need to have insurance available in your sixties or seventies in order to pay any estate taxes or funeral expenses that will be due on a nonliquid estate. You may have a closely held business or some significant nonliquid assets that you want to pass on to your heirs. If you take the approach of buying term, at some point the term insurance will become cost-prohibitive and you will no longer have it, thus reducing your options. This points to the second reason to have a long-term insurance plan: flexibility. In your thirties and forties you do not know what your situation will be when you are in your sixties. Having a cornerstone of permanent insurance available at that stage in your life is simply wise planning—looking down the road and counting the cost.

Therefore, *the issue of how long you need insurance is difficult to resolve, because no one knows what the future holds.* But if the need is strictly short-term and will never be any longer than that, then the obvious solution is term insurance. However, if there is an outside chance that estate taxes must be paid or if you want to build in some flexibility for long-term planning, then you should consider some type of permanent insurance for part of your coverage as soon as you can afford it.

What Type of Insurance Product Do You Need?

Although insurance comes in hundreds of "wrappers," there are basically five different types of insurance policies. These are term (such as annual renewable term and guaranteed level premium 5-, 10-, 15-, 20-, and 30-year products), traditional whole life, a hybrid product (a combination of whole life and term), universal life, and variable life.

Term Life Insurance

Annual renewable term life insurance provides the maximum insurance coverage for the lowest initial premiums, with premiums increasing annually. The premium costs at older ages (age sixty to life expectancy) are prohibitive and make it difficult to maintain this type of policy until death. This product does not allow any flexibility in premium payments to meet changing circumstances. The obvious advantage of this type of coverage is the low initial cost, while the not-so-obvious disadvantage is the high cost during the later years. Level-premium term policies provide the benefit of locking in a premium for a certain period of time, for example, twenty years. In general, young families will provide the majority of their insurance needs with term insurance. I recommend locking in your term insurance with a guaranteed level premium for fifteen to twenty years when you need the maximum life insurance protection (when children are young).

Traditional Whole Life Insurance

This product is more expensive initially than a term policy because of the level premiums, the cash value buildup, and higher commission costs to the agent. In a sense, the insurance owner overpays in the early years in order to underpay (or not pay) in later years. It is this aspect of a whole life policy that gives rise to the accumulation of cash value in the policy. This "forced savings" aspect of a whole life policy has been a controversial subject for many years. While many people indicate they do not need to do this, my experience has shown that most people do a poor job of saving for the future, so this aspect of a whole life policy may be helpful. Even though the policy contract may require premiums to be paid for a certain length of time (that is, one's lifetime), the policy may be paid up much sooner with the use of dividends. The primary disadvantage of a whole life policy is the high outlay of premiums required in the early years. Although term life insurance is more cost effective and should be used for most of your life insurance needs, I think that some of your insurance protection can be met through whole life.

The Hybrid (Whole Life/Term Combination)

This product has some characteristics of both whole life and term insurance. The premiums are typically lower than a traditional whole life product but higher than a term policy. There is a buildup of cash value on these policies but at a lower rate than on the whole life policies. The percentage of whole life versus term insurance initially purchased will dictate the amount of the premium and the number of years you have to pay. Each year the dividend will automatically buy paid-up insurance to replace a portion of the term insurance; over a period of time the term is entirely replaced. In many cases the owner can vary the level of term insurance initially and then add money to the contract with very little or no commission taken out, thereby improving the overall performance of this policy.

Universal Life

This type of insurance has as its primary advantage the aspect of flexibility. It is flexible with regard to the death benefit as well as the premiums paid and the ability to withdraw cash from the policy. Another possible advantage of a universal policy is that the public can more readily understand it. This contract is essentially a combination of an investment vehicle and term insurance. The insured makes premium payments to the contract, which are credited with an interest rate on a monthly basis. Certain charges are taken out from the fund on a monthly basis. These include mortality costs and other administrative expenses.

A word of caution about universal life: The same feature that could be an advantage of this contract may become a disadvantage. The ability to vary the premium payments may put the insured in a position of having under funded the contract in later years and seeing his coverage expire. This is particularly true when an agent or company has projected a high rate of return through the life of the policy, when in fact the economic environment dictates that a lower interest rate is actually credited to his account during many of these years. Besides being able to vary the face amount of coverage and the premium payments, the policy also allows for cash withdrawals without actually borrowing on the funds.

Variable Life

As if insurance were not confusing enough, a product known as variable life has been marketed to the consumer with increasing frequency. Variable life insurance is similar to whole life in that the premium payments are level, and there is generally a minimum guaranteed death benefit. Unlike whole life policies, however, variable life policies permit the policyholder to allocate a portion of each premium payment to one or more investment options after a deduction for expense and mortality charges. The investment options are typically mutual funds inside the whole life product.

Traditional whole life and universal life policies typically have a fixed dividend or interest rate credited to their accounts on an annual basis. In the last decade, as interest rates have declined, the interest rates credited to these products have also decreased. This has resulted in the current cash values being significantly less than the projections that were made when they were sold five or ten years ago. At the same time that interest rates have been declining, the stock market has been achieving double-digit returns. Variable life appears attractive since the cash value built up inside these policies, if projected at the historical earning rates of the stock market, can outperform other insurance products.

Should you purchase a variable life insurance product? Perhaps— if you are a knowledgeable investor and understand the downside risk of the stock market, which could cause the cash value of your contract to decline. Second, you would need to have an extremely long-term perspective, since the near-term volatility of the stock market could give you false hopes or false fears about your policy. Generally, I don't recommend mixing investments with insurance. Life insurance has traditionally been associated with protection. Variable life is often sold as an investment product. Be sure that you fully understand the risks and rewards of purchasing a variable life product.

In order for you to determine what kind of insurance you need, it's important for you to step back and look at these insurance products from an overall perspective. This will mean asking the questions, how much do I need? (see the Insurance Needs Analysis, chart 14-A). How long do I need it, and how much can I afford? Once you answer these questions, the appropriate product should become obvious.

For long-term needs, I recommend that you go with a financially strong mutual company with a good agent who will be around to service the product ten or twenty years down the road. The product type will depend on available cash, but the traditional whole life may be the best choice, although the other products mentioned certainly merit consideration.

Short-term and intermediate-term needs can be met through term insurance, but here again I would recommend a higher-quality company over the lowest-cost term. This is because of convertibility, not insurability. (This is a key factor, because a significant portion of term insurance is converted, and being with a quality company is a plus at the time of conversion.)

Insurance is a wise cornerstone of a complete financial plan, and it's necessary for peace of mind in the family unit. Although the marketplace can be confusing, thinking through the issues raised in this chapter should help you arrive at a sound decision. However, certain questions about insurance are common. I will address those before discussing the matter of estate planning.

Insurance Questions and Answers

What if I cannot afford the amount of insurance I need?

In this case, get all the insurance you can for the dollars available. A second step would be to make sure your family has a written plan concerning the use of the insurance and alternatives for additional financial help to secure additional dollars for insurance or upon the premature death of a spouse (spouse working, family help, where to get counsel, etc.).

Does a nonworking spouse need insurance?

Yes! If you can afford it. Compute the cost of replacing the service this spouse provides (for example: child care, more meals out, higher dry cleaning costs, house cleaning costs), if these cannot or do not want to be provided by the remaining spouse. If the insurance funds are limited, they belong on the breadwinner of the family, but don't ever leave a spouse uninsured for life insurance if at all possible. Funeral expenses alone may cost up to $10,000. If the family is dependent on both spouses' incomes, then there may have to be some allocation to insurance for both. The least expensive way to do this is to include coverage for both as a part of the insurance coverage for the spouse earning the greatest income.

Do the children need insurance?

Again, if insurance funds are limited, provide insurance for the breadwinner first. The purpose of insurance is provision. The children are not part of a family's provision.

There are five basic reasons for having insurance on a child:

1. To provide guaranteed insurability. This is a major point used in selling insurance for children. The idea implanted is that the child needs insurance in case he or she becomes disabled prior to becoming an adult and thus would not qualify for insurance. The probability of this is very small.

2. To give them direction into a quality company at an early age.

3. For cash accumulation that can be used in purchasing other insurance policies at a later time.

4. Low rates at an early start.

5. To provide for unexpected funeral expenses.

I personally bought a relatively small whole life policy on each of my children. My intention was to provide them with some life insurance in case they had health problems and would not be insurable. The policy offered the option to buy additional insurance at various intervals as they grew. When the kids were on their own, I gave them these policies to let them decide whether to keep them or not. With your children, let your budget and your priorities be your guide in determining how much, if any, insurance should be purchased.

I would not recommend using insurance as a primary way to save for education. Other tax-advantaged ways exist to save for higher education.

Is whole life or insurance with "savings" always a bad buy?

No, just usually more expensive. The economic aspect of insurance savings needs to be weighed carefully against other savings alternatives. Also, a long-term perspective may dictate a "permanent" insurance product.

When is whole life insurance a good investment?

When it disciplines the insured to save money he or she might not otherwise have saved, or after a product has been held more than five years. (Older permanent policies may be good investments even though the death benefit may be somewhat smaller than with new products.)

When do I not need insurance?

When your investment assets reach the point that the income derived from them, plus other income that will not change in the event of death, will meet the provision you are responsible for. Until that time, insurance becomes an umbrella of protection to provide the needed resource in the event that you die before meeting your financial goals.

Retirement might be such a time. At retirement the income should be set. Its source might be Social Security, pension plans, annuities, or investments. If the spouse's needs are also met after the death of the provider, then there would not be a need for insurance to supply additional provision. There would also have to be no anticipated estate tax or liquidity needs.

At the other extreme, a young single person with no family or support responsibilities would have no need for insurance. An exception perhaps would be to have enough insurance so that burial costs or debt repayment would not present a burden to anyone.

Should I cash in my whole life insurance policy that has a high cash value and convert it to term?

It depends, but honestly I am reluctant to advise anyone to cancel any existing life insurance. Simply put, I have never seen any widow or family member complain about the deceased having too much life insurance! If you have had your whole life insurance policy for many years with a good company, you are probably earning a relatively good yield for the low level of risk. You may be better off to keep it. I would recommend that you work through the specific facts and circumstances with a financial adviser. Your adviser can help you see how much life insurance you need and help hold you accountable to invest the cash value wisely (rather than spend it) if you decide to cancel the policy.

Do insurance needs change?

They certainly do. Because of this, you should perform a periodic review of insurance with respect to your overall financial position and provision requirements. For example, when a man marries, he is responsible to provide for his wife. This may precipitate an insurance need. When children come along, the need for insurance may increase because of the need to assure that they are educated and then given an opportunity to make a living. Also, adequate capital is needed so the wife does not have to go to work and can spend time training the posterity. As children gain independence, the provision needs may decrease.

Other factors may prompt an insurance reevaluation:

❖ A significant rise in inflation

❖ Increased income or lifestyle costs

❖ Heavy personal or business debt obligations

❖ A change in estate liquidity needs

❖ Long-term flexibility

Is insurance scriptural?

There is no mention in Scripture of insurance. The assumption would therefore be that it is not unscriptural. Scripture does emphasize trusting God. If insurance replaces trust in God, that is unscriptural. Scripture also emphasizes wise planning and providing for family members. The key is to have a balanced attitude toward it.

If I foresee a long-term need for insurance, should I purchase whole life insurance?

A long-term need means you have a need for insurance beyond age sixty-five. Most likely this would be for estate liquidity purposes or perhaps to provide flexibility in planning at that time in life. In this case, whole life insurance, with its level premiums and lower costs (assuming it was purchased at a much younger age) would be the preferable product.

What about mortgage life insurance?

Mortgage life insurance is purchased for the exclusive purpose of paying off the house debt when the homeowner (borrower) dies. It is actually a decreasing term type of insurance because, as the debt is decreased, the insurance company's liability is decreased. These policies are frequently more expensive than yearly renewable term products after the first several years. Most mortgage insurance is very expensive when reduced to the dollar cost per $1,000 of insurance base. This is especially the case if it is purchased through a mortgage company or bank. The alternative is to increase your existing life insurance to provide this coverage (if it is not already provided through a previous needs analysis) or to purchase a separate decreasing term life insurance policy for this purchase and cancel it when the mortgage is paid.

Do I need credit life insurance on my loans?

As with mortgage insurance, credit insurance is very expensive. It is not recommended for that reason alone. In many cases, however, the lender as a condition of the loan requires it. In that case, your only options are to find another lender; pay the price; save and pay cash; or forego the purchase.

Your Insurance Needs Analysis includes provision for debt payoff. Since debt varies, you may want to make a provision for an average amount of debt. Of course, the simplest way to deal with this area is to live debt free as a part of your financial plan.

Estate Planning

Estate planning is planning for your death so that your family and financial resources are distributed and cared for in accordance with your objectives.

A well thought-out estate plan will include not only a will, but also life insurance, correctly owned and with proper beneficiary designations, property deeded appropriately, survivors instructed in both written form and orally as to wishes and desires, proper and easily located records, advisors properly selected and instructed, and perhaps many other things. As can be seen, an estate plan is a very comprehensive plan for death, when planning is no longer possible. Therefore, it must be well documented and totally complete. Unfortunately, it is estimated that 50 percent of Americans don't even have a will, let alone the other elements necessary for a complete and proper estate plan.

Reasons Given for Not Planning Your Estate

"*My estate is too small.*" An estate may be too small to have estate taxes due on it, but there is more to an estate plan than just the tax aspects. Appointing a guardian to care for any children is far too important a matter to be left to a total stranger. In addition, a relatively simple will can avoid many of the administrative costs associated with death.

When considering the size of an estate, many people forget that life insurance can add significantly to an estate size and may cause not only tax problems, but other types of problems as well.

One other reason for planning the estate rather than leaving it for the state court system to handle is that any particular personal effects you want to go to specific relatives or friends must be designated in a will. Otherwise, your intentions mean nothing, and the law of the land will determine who gets what.

"*It's too expensive.*" Many people are "penny-wise and pound-foolish" and think that a will and other actions necessary for proper estate planning are too expensive. First of all, that thought may be an assumption and not a fact. My recommendation is to get an estimate or several estimates from those qualified to prepare the documents. On the other hand, probably no price is too great to pay for making it easier on friends and family who have never had to experience life without you.

"I don't have enough time." The underlying reason for this statement is probably a fear of death. Many people superstitiously believe that as long as they don't prepare a will, they won't die. Also, many just avoid talking about death. It is a very uncomfortable topic of discussion for them. Again, with certainty, everyone will die, and for the Christian to be superstitious about his or her death is to have a poor understanding of the promises God has made in the Bible.

"I'm not certain about what I want to do." Because estate planning can be a very complex and certainly unfamiliar topic, many do not know how to go about setting those objectives. This is a legitimate concern. However, God promises to provide us the wisdom that we need (see James 1:5), and when we are planning for the future, we need God's wisdom for certain.

Also, no estate plan should be written in concrete. The design should always be flexible since our needs, desires, and circumstances change over time.

Estate Planning Objectives

Distribution of Financial Resources

There are only four alternatives available for the allocation of your financial resources: family and friends, charity, taxes, and expenses. You should plan this allocation after spending time with God to minimize the shrinkage from unnecessary expenses. The potential for conflict is great when it comes to predetermining priorities. I promise that the conflict you face in making these decisions is less than the conflict others will have making them for you, without you. My challenge to the people that I speak to is to list these four alternatives and then to put either a percent or a dollar amount next to each one in order to quantify how they want their estate distributed. Generally speaking, if you can quantify where you want your estate to ultimately end up, then the estate plan can be drafted accordingly. The problem is that most people do not know or will not decide how they want their estate to be allocated.

Obviously, within the categories of family and friends and charity, there can be many alternatives.

Provide Estate Liquidity

Liquidity always provides flexibility. If an estate has any size at all, flexibility is needed to provide for the transition period immediately after one's death until assets can be transferred, retitled, and released. Sometimes this transition period lasts several years. In addition, liquidity helps prevent the sale of nonliquid assets in perhaps an unfavorable economic environment when they would lose or have a loss due to decline in their true value. Liquidity is also needed to pay taxes, if any are due, and to make it easier to distribute an estate among several beneficiaries.

One of the most nonliquid assets that can typically have significant size is the value in a closely held business. By planning for the proper amount of liquidity, a closely held business can continue to function and provide the security needed for both the employees and owners. Insufficient liquidity can force the sale of a business at perhaps an inopportune time.

Provide for Ease of Management and Administration of Estate

Sometimes a wife is left after the death of her husband with no experience in managing assets. She undoubtedly would have the ability to do so with proper training, but suddenly she is overwhelmed with the responsibility for more money than she has ever managed from life insurance and other assets. However, to select an executor or trustee other than a spouse may mean that control for the management and administration of the estate passes to a nonfamily member.

The person doing the estate planning must provide for the administration and management of the estate, taking into account the experience and ability of those appointed to this role. My advice is typically to name the spouse as executor and trustee because he or she can always hire any counsel that is needed to manage the estate's assets properly. When control is given to a corporate entity, such as a bank or a nonfamily member, then control literally passes at the point of death, and that too becomes a poor stewardship decision in retrospect. Story after story can be told of widows at the mercy of unsympathetic former business partners, bank trust officers, family friends, or even other family members.

I recently heard such a story after speaking at a conference. I had mentioned the estate planning principle "Never use a trust because of a lack of trust." A recent widow came up to me after the presentation and confirmed this principle.

Her husband had died suddenly. She did not know the value of his estate or their estate plans. Much to her surprise, her husband's assets and life insurance were worth $8,000,000. Much to her dismay, the entire $8,000,000 was left to a trust at a local bank. The trust provided for her lifestyle needs during her lifetime and named her two daughters as the beneficiaries. Every time she needed to obtain money for a significant purchase, she felt a bit degraded to justify to the bank trust officer why she needed another vehicle or to go on a mission trip. She had to defend her lifestyle and provide support for any principal withdrawal to the trust officer. She felt even more hurt because her husband didn't trust her to share the estate plans or with the use of the money for her own benefit.

I recommend that all parties affected by an estate plan review it together so their responsibilities can be clearly delineated by the one who is leaving the estate. While there is still opportunity, the individual should articulate his or her desires in front of all the family members and friends who are affected. Admittedly, this is something that is very, very rarely done—it never seems important until it is too late! In order to do this, I recommend a *family conference*. Appendix A contains an explanation of the purpose of this conference and how to conduct one.

I always recommend that a husband honor his absolute obligation to train his wife while he is alive to manage whatever God has entrusted to the two of them. Otherwise, she has been effectively disinherited.

I remember visiting with a man who wanted me to help him plan his estate. He literally had several million dollars in cash that constituted his entire estate. He had no debts, a great marriage, and a desire to leave his estate ultimately to the Lord's work. As we were discussing the estate plan, he advised me that his wife had no idea how much they were worth. She trusted him implicitly with their financial situation and never questioned his decisions. However, when he described his intentions of giving away his entire estate, I asked him how his wife was going to feel when the will was read and she realized that she had had no part in determining where the millions were to go. They had several children, all of whom were at that time doing well spiritually and financially, but circumstances could change and his wife would have no opportunity to provide for any of the children or grandchildren under the proposed estate plan.

When I confronted him with his wife's potential feelings, he immediately saw the error in his thinking, went home, and shared his plans with his wife. Together they developed an estate plan that provided a bit more flexibility for her, but still accomplished the objectives he had for the ultimate distribution of the estate. That could have been a very tragic story had the man not included his wife in determining the objectives for the estate.

Provide for Care of Immediate Family

When children are young, guardianship in the event of the death of both parents must be addressed. Also, the education needs, the physical needs, and the mental or emotional needs of children may change with time. For example, a proper estate plan must be in place for a physically or mentally handicapped child. Older persons may plan to provide for the special needs of their grandchildren.

Providing for the care of the family also means that you have as an objective to maintain the lifestyle of the surviving spouse for some time period.

Provide for Grown Children

There is a fine line between provision and protection. We are to provide for our families, but not to the extent that they have no opportunity to trust God for work in their lives. Many children—and even young adults—have been ruined by overindulgent parents who left everything to them without considering the ramifications of doing this in their children's lives.

It is a parent's responsibility, according to Proverbs 22:6, to "train up a child in the way he should go." That responsibility does not end when the child leaves home, and if the parents have failed in the training, then I suggest that they not compound that failure by leaving financial resources that protect the children from God's dealing with them in their adult lives.

I also believe that a parent should recognize differences in children—differences due to age, gender, temperament, their demonstrated ability to handle money, their spiritual commitment, their spiritual maturity, their known or unknown marriage partners, and their children. It is a parent and grandparent's responsibility to entrust God's resources to children only if they have demonstrated the ability to handle those resources in a manner that would be pleasing to Him who is the owner of all.

If a parent entrusts God's resources to a slothful child, it is no different than giving those resources to any slothful stranger. Just because you have a child does not make the child the automatic beneficiary of your estate. The scriptural precedent is that if basic needs are met, the money should be left to those who have demonstrated sound stewardship. According to Ecclesiastes 7:11–12, if we leave money to someone to whom we have not left wisdom, it can be a devastating situation. I believe that more prayer, wisdom, and decisiveness are needed in meeting this objective of providing for grown children than any other estate planning area. Obviously, great emotion and perhaps tradition are involved. Here again, this is something that can and should be discussed in a family conference forum. Better to discuss unequal distributions to children while you are alive than to run the risk of bitterness toward you after you are dead.

Provide for Charity

Unless you plan for charitable giving in your estate plan and put it into words in your will, it won't happen. Many sources confirm that very few people include charitable giving in their wills. The government doesn't say, "He gave to his church all his life. Surely he wanted to give to it upon death." Because any charitable gifts given at death are a deduction from the total estate for estate tax purposes, all charitable giving at death reduces the estate taxes payable. The trade-off almost always becomes one between giving to family members and the government or giving to charity, and it is never an easy question to handle. My own belief is that the majority of charitable giving should be done while the income is being earned rather than delayed until death. After death, you have no more control over the property anyway, and it is not actually giving in the sense of giving up anything. Giving at death, however, is an opportunity to continue having an effect for Christ on earth while you are enjoying your new relationship with Him in heaven.

One means for your estate to continue to give to charity after your death is through a charitable trust described later in this chapter.

Provide Testimony

When my mother-in-law died, along with her will was a note to her children expressing that her greatest desire was for them to accept Jesus Christ as their personal Savior and to spend eternity with her. She was sure of her relationship with Him. A will can provide a public record of your Christian testimony, not only for your children but also for anyone else who reads that document, including attorneys, judges, accountants, and perhaps grandchildren and great-grandchildren. Obviously, without a will, you do not have that written document of public testimony.

Provide for Future Planning Flexibility

Because circumstances and desires change over time, very little of an estate plan should be "written in concrete." In other words, irrevocable decisions need to be postponed, if possible, until death. The typical estate plan does not come into being until death. However, when an estate gets to be fairly sizeable, certain irrevocable decisions, such as property ownership, may have to be made. My recommendation is that all such decisions be made only when absolutely necessary and beneficial.

Estate Planning Fundamentals

Where There's a Will . . .

Let's start with the basic tool in the wealth transfer process: your will. Your will is the foundational cornerstone of an estate plan. It is a written, witnessed document that defines your final wishes and desires regarding many things, including property distribution. A person who dies with a will is called one who dies testate. A person who dies without a will dies intestate, and the laws of intestacy apply.

The laws of intestacy differ from state to state, but in general, if one dies intestate, that person gives the state government the right to determine:

❖ The control of their financial resources,

❖ The distribution of those resources,

❖ The choice of executor,

❖ The choice of a guardian for minor children,

❖ The ability to waive fiduciary bonds, and

❖ The right to authorize a business continuation plan.

On the other hand, a person who dies with a will retains the following:

❖ The control and the use of their assets,

❖ The distribution of those assets,

❖ The bequeathing of specific personal possessions to loved ones,

❖ The choice of the executor,

❖ The choice of a guardian for minor children,

❖ The right to waive fiduciary bonds (such bonds can be expensive), and

❖ The right to set up various trusts to reduce estate taxes and probate costs.

Many Americans don't have a will. Survey after survey reveals that the number of procrastinators ranges from 50–60 percent. An important step for all good stewards is to implement the basic tool of a will. Your good intentions or your prayerful consideration of the wealth transfer process won't get the job done. In many states, the surviving spouse has no say in the matter if there is no will. Your estate becomes subject to the responsibility and function of the court system.

What Do You Put in Your Will?

A will is where you make certain appointments and leave property to certain people or organizations. This is where you describe any specific bequests made after consideration of your transfer decision. As part of implementing your treatment decision, you would describe specific bequests to individual children and grandchildren. You can even get very specific in a will to specify that the china dishes go to your daughter rather than your daughters-in-law.

Many people erroneously believe that if they have a small estate, everything will go to the surviving spouse. Therefore, they see no reason to have a will. On the contrary, your assets may not all go to the spouse; they may be allocated among the children and the spouse. The spouse may not have much say over how the children's portion is managed, either.

You cannot simply tell your family members what you want done with your property after your death. Oral expressions made during your lifetime have no legal standing when you are dead. I urge you to have a will that is executed (signed and witnessed properly) and valid under your particular state's laws.

Naming Names

An important appointment made in your will can improve your peace of mind. In your will, you will appoint an executor and a guardian (if your children are minors). The executor is responsible for assuming the property belonging to the estate, safeguarding and insuring the estate property during the period of estate settlement, and temporarily managing the estate while the estate is being settled. The person you designate will be involved in paying the estate taxes and expenses, accounting for the estate administration, and making distribution of the net estate to the heirs. The duties of the executor can be very time-consuming, frustrating, and complicated. To a surviving spouse, it can be overwhelming. If you have more than one adult child, choosing one of them as executor could possibly sow seeds for mistrust and resentment among the children. You may choose in your will a qualified individual (such as an accountant or lawyer or trusted friend) or corporate trust company (such as a bank) to assist or fulfill all these duties.

The *guardian* is someone you would trust to take over the care and upbringing of your minor children if something were to happen to both of you. Consider the financial situation of the potential guardian; his or her health, age, and spiritual maturity; and the compatibility of that person's values with yours. Include in your will alternate choices of guardians. Don't forget to obtain permission from any named guardians and executors. Without a will, if both parents should die in a common accident, the court will determine the guardian(s) of minor-aged children.

Does having a will distribute all my wealth according to my wishes?

No, not necessarily. Some assets pass outside of your will. Check your beneficiary designations on 401(k)s, IRAs, annuities, and life insurance.

You may have taken great pains to word your will, name heirs, and get your will completed. If so, I commend you. But don't miss something that may not appear obvious—naming beneficiaries. The total value of your IRAs, 401(k)s, and life insurance will pass directly to the named beneficiaries *regardless* of what is in your will. For many people, the majority of their wealth may be passed directly to beneficiaries.

Will I have to pay estate taxes or the so-called "death" taxes?

Since 1916, the federal government of the United States has levied taxes on estates. The original and continuing official rationale is that the estate tax prevents the concentration of wealth. In reality, the estate tax is another means of raising revenue for a government eager to spend it. If its aim were to prevent concentration of wealth, then the tax would be based on what each heir receives rather than what the deceased person owned. The estate tax is the same on the deceased person's wealth whether one person receives it or thirty people receive it.

In a technical sense, you do not pay the estate tax. You have to die before it applies. Your estate will pay the tax. So, your heirs would receive fewer assets. Here's the equation: Your total assets owned at death minus any estate taxes owed equals the amount available for your heirs. The irritating aspect of the estate tax is that much of your wealth has already been taxed for income taxes when you earned it. Let's say that you worked as an employee for forty years and diligently saved and invested your earnings. You paid income tax throughout your working life on the wages earned and the interest and dividends earned. If you did a great job of saving and investing to build an account of $2,000,000, then your estate may have to pay estate taxes too—at very high rates (minimum of 18 percent rising very quickly to a top rate of 48 percent).

Notice in the last sentence that I said your estate "may" have to pay estate taxes. Despite the bad news that wealth may be potentially taxed twice, the good news is that everyone receives a standard credit from estate and gift taxes. (I have added gift taxes because the estate and gift taxes are related to each other. You can't escape estate taxes by giving away everything—because gift taxes would likely then apply.) This standard credit is technically called the *unified credit*. It is an estate and gift tax credit allowed by law to offset any estate or gift tax due on any transfers of property that are taxed. The amount of the unified credit effective for 2004 is $555,800. This credit will offset the tax on an estate totaling $1.5 million. So, you can give away or transfer to individuals up to $1.5 million without triggering estate or gift taxes. Accountants and lawyers refer to this amount as the technical term exemption equivalent, but I will refer to it as the Lifetime Exemption.

For many years, the Lifetime Exemption was $600,000. In response to their constituents, Congress raised the Lifetime Exemption effective in 2000. The Tax Act of 2001 implemented a gradual phase-in of increasing it to $3.5 million in the year 2009. Effective for 2010, the estate tax is entirely repealed. Then, in a strange result of political compromise, the estate tax comes back! And it reverts back to the rates in place during 2002 when the Lifetime Exemption was $1,000,000. So, now you must choose a tax-effective year to die!

I mention the future planned chaos in the federal estate tax code to point out that these rates and approaches to taxation are in constant change. The concepts and ideas presented in this chapter will likely continue to apply despite changes in the estate and gift tax rates and in the Lifetime Exemption. Congress and the president may radically change the nature and amount of the estate tax rules. Recognizing this reality of change should result in your periodic review of your wealth transfer plans with a competent tax professional. I will use a Lifetime Exemption amount of $1.5 million for illustrative purpose in the remainder of this chapter.

Let me sum up the basic aspects of estate taxes we have learned so far with the example of Widow Smith. Her estimated assets available at her death total $1.3 million. This includes her house, CDs, investments, IRA, and the life insurance amount her beneficiaries will receive. She made no significant gifts to individuals during her lifetime. Widow Smith's estate will owe zero in estate taxes. She will not even have to file an estate tax return because the total value of her estate is less than the Lifetime Exemption of $1.5 million. You may already feel relieved if your estate value is well under the current Lifetime Exemption.

How do estate taxes apply if I leave everything to my spouse?

You can leave an unlimited amount of property to your spouse and your estate will not have to pay any estate taxes. This sounds too good to be true, right? It is true, but there may be a trap. Let me explain further and use the concept of Lifetime Exemption we discussed in the last section.

A *marital deduction* means property that one spouse can transfer to the living spouse at his or her death without paying an estate tax. The amount is unlimited. This can enable a person to avoid all estate tax at the death of the first spouse. The same idea applies to lifetime gifts. The *marital gift exclusion* allows one spouse to transfer an unlimited amount to the other spouse before death without paying a gift transfer tax.

As an illustration, let's say that Tom dies and left his land holdings worth $5,000,000 to his wife, Gerri. Because of the unlimited marital deduction, no estate tax is due upon his death. Sounds good so far, but the trap comes at Gerri's death. Let's further assume that she suffered from extreme grief from Tom's death and died the following month. Her estate will be taxed. How much of Gerri's estate will be taxable? The taxable portion will be $3.5 million ($5,000,000 less her Lifetime Exemption of $1.5 million).

Remember that the Lifetime Exemption applies to *each* person. Tom has $1.5 million and Gerri has $1.5 million that they can exempt from estate taxes. The Lifetime Exemption dies with you. So, Tom did not benefit from his $1.5 million Lifetime Exemption. He transferred everything to his wife, Gerri. No estate taxes were owed because of the unlimited marital deduction. He didn't use the Lifetime Exemption, it died with him, and his family lost the benefit of it. We will look at tools and techniques to preserve the value of the Lifetime Exemption in a following section.

How do gifts affect estate taxes?

The estate and gift tax laws state that any gifts made during the last three years of a person's life must be counted in the deceased person's estate. Gifts are still considered, on paper at least, as part of a person's estate and are taxed if given within the last three years of life. These laws then effectively limit the "deathbed" gifts or signing over of deeds to reduce estate taxes.

Another important concept with gifts is the *annual gift exclusion.* The annual gift exclusion is simply the dollar amount of an asset that can be transferred every year from any person to any other person or persons free from any gift taxes and without using up any of your unified credit. As of 2004, the annual gift exclusion amount is $11,000. For many years the amount was $10,000 per person.

Remember that the estate and gift taxation system works together; it is unified. If John makes a single gift of $500,000 in stock to his son, then gift tax is due (because this is more than the $11,000 annual exclusion amount). John can pay the gift tax in the year the gift was made. Or, John may choose to not pay gift tax now, but he will use up $489,000 of his Lifetime Exemption for estate taxes. If John's total estate is expected to be less than $1.5 million, he can safely use up some of his unified credit because his estate will not owe estate taxes.

Is it true that life insurance proceeds count as part of my estate and may be subject to estate taxes?

Yes—if you own the policy. I understand that it may seem odd that your estate will be taxed on something you never received. Life insurance proceeds made payable to your beneficiaries will be added back to your estate for purposes of the estate taxes.

Let's use an extreme example to illustrate this fact. Barbara had $100,000 in a CD and a house worth $150,000. Therefore, her assets owned before death total $250,000. She owned a life insurance policy for $2,000,000 with her only daughter named as beneficiary. Upon Barbara's death, her estate will be valued at $2,250,000. The taxable portion will be $750,000 (the total estate value less the Lifetime Exemption).

Many people wisely use life insurance to provide liquidity at the time of death, to provide for survivors, and perhaps to pay estate taxes. However, keep in mind that, unless the ownership is properly structured, the life insurance will be added back to your estate's value when computing the estate tax due. (Stay tuned for a tip to structure this properly.)

Turning these basics into five ways to save a half a million in taxes!

Now that you have some facts, let's see how they might apply. Although the estate tax seems onerous, the good news is that it is the easiest tax to legally avoid. Minimizing your tax is a valid goal of a good steward, but it is not the most important aim. Remember the tools principle: Estate planning tools and techniques help you accomplish objectives, but are not the objective. If your objective is to give generously to charity and to your adult children, then minimizing taxes supports your objective. Less to the government means more to charity and to your children.

After you complete the earlier wealth transfer decisions presented so far and if the value of your estimated estate is likely to be more than $1.5 million, then consider the following ideas to save literally hundreds of thousands of dollars in estate taxes. These are simple steps. They are not the most advanced steps, but the K.I.S.S. Principle (of course, the acronym for this principle is from the saying "keep it simple, stupid") reminds us that we do not need to be more complex than necessary to reach our objectives and to minimize taxes.

1. *Maximize the Lifetime Exemption by retitling property between the spouses and passing some property to eventual heirs upon the death of the first spouse.* Because each person gets a Lifetime Exemption ($1.5 million in 2004), use that exemption. Instead of transferring all your assets to your spouse, transfer an amount equal to the Lifetime Exemption to your adult children or some organization upon your death. The benefit: Your eventual heirs will get assets earlier and there is less property in the estate of the second spouse. Less property means less tax.

Let's revisit the example of Tom and Gerri that I previously used when explaining the marital deduction. Tom had a total of $5,000,000 in land holdings. These properties were held jointly with his wife. If Tom had a few properties that totaled $1.5 million in value, he could change the title so he owned it individually. In his will, Tom could have these properties he individually owns transferred to his children. Then, the $1.5 million in assets transferred would be offset by the $1.5 Lifetime Exemption resulting in no estate taxes. After his wife, Gerri, died, her estate of $3.5 million would be able to deduct the Lifetime Exemption of $1.5 million. Only $2,000,000 of her estate would be taxed. Thus, each spouse was able to use the Lifetime Exemption. Voila! Tax savings of more than $500,000.

While this idea may work in some cases, there may be practical problems. What if the assets are not easily divisible into a portion equaling the Lifetime Exemption? What if the surviving spouse needs the income from the assets to live on? These practical challenges lead to the second idea—another way to maximize the Lifetime Exemption.

2. *Maximize the Lifetime Exemption by using a marital (or A-B) trust.* The most common type of will, and the simplest, is the "I love you" or "simple" will. This type of will simply states that the first spouse to die leaves everything to the surviving spouse using the unlimited marital deduction. This means that if all assets are left to your spouse, no estate tax is due upon the death of the first spouse. This is a very attractive will for an estate that is under $1.5 million. As I have already pointed out, substantial taxes could result at the surviving spouse's death if the estate is over $1.5 million. To avoid this large, potential tax problem at the death of the survivor, the second common type of will is used.

The second type of will is the A-B will. This type of will sets up one or two trusts. The objective is to keep a portion of the assets in the estate of the first spouse to die to utilize the Lifetime Exemption. (Sometimes the resulting trust is called a bypass trust because the principal bypasses the spouse.)

For example, this type of will, instead of leaving everything to the spouse, will say something like "I leave everything to my spouse [outright or in trust] except the maximum amount I can keep in my estate and not be subject to estate tax [which, of course, could be as much as $1.5 million]. The amount kept in my estate will go into trust for the benefit of my spouse." A trust is simply a separate taxable entity that is set up during life or through a will to enable an individual to accomplish different desired planning objectives.

If the first amount is left outright, you will have one trust. If it is left in trust, you end up with two trusts. Refer to figure 14.2 on page 227. (The legalese will be much different from what I have stated, but in essence that is what happens.)

A-B Will Example with Two Trusts

Figure 14.2

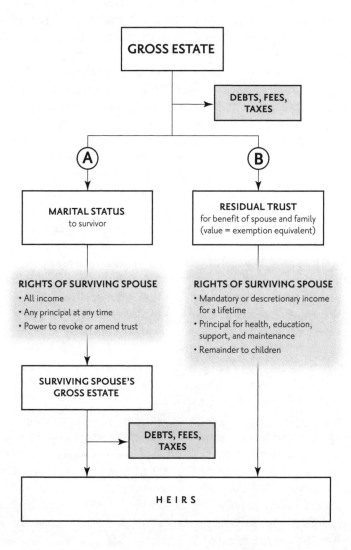

GROSS ESTATE

DEBTS, FEES, TAXES

A

B

MARITAL STATUS
to survivor

RESIDUAL TRUST
for benefit of spouse and family
(value = exemption equivalent)

RIGHTS OF SURVIVING SPOUSE
• All income
• Any principal at any time
• Power to revoke or amend trust

RIGHTS OF SURVIVING SPOUSE
• Mandatory or descretionary income
for a lifetime
• Principal for health, education,
support, and maintenance
• Remainder to children

SURVIVING SPOUSE'S
GROSS ESTATE

DEBTS, FEES, TAXES

HEIRS

The terms of the trust that will hold the assets left in the decedent's estate (the first to die) are then written in such a way that the survivor has "virtual" ownership of the assets in the trust. In other words, he or she can get income and principal from the trust as needed. Another benefit of the trust is that it provides the surviving spouse with the assistance of a trustee in managing the assets.

By the way, the *trustee* is responsible for managing the estate left in trust in accordance with the terms of your will. The trustee could be a corporation, such as a bank, or an individual. I typically recommend having an individual trustee because he or she is likely to be more responsive to the needs of the surviving spouse. This does not negate the fact that in many specific cases a bank trustee is preferred. Professional counsel should be sought in making this trustee selection.

The executor and the trustee can be one and the same. The trustee does not necessarily need to be knowledgeable in financial affairs, although that may help. Trustees usually seek outside expert financial advice from someone in the business (trust department, financial planning firm). The key concerns in appointing both the executor and trustee are the following: Are they trustworthy? Will they be sensitive to the needs of your family? Do they have integrity? Do they have wisdom not to be taken advantage of?

The A-B will and marital trusts are a common technique. Although there is a bit of setup work, you can save well over $500,000 in taxes, your spouse still has the benefits of the income, and assets are safeguarded for the eventual heirs.

3. *Begin giving gifts now to individual heirs to take advantage of the annual gift exclusion.* If your estate may be subject to taxes, an added reason to give now is the reduction in your estate and, consequently, the reduction in taxes. Every $11,000 gift saves between $4,000 and $5,000 in taxes. Everyone wins—except the IRS.

The exclusion provides for an attractive way to remove assets from one's estate with no legal fees or complication—a great example of the K.I.S.S. Principle. For an illustration of how this can work in fairly large numbers, let's assume that Jay and Carol have plenty of income to live on through pensions and rental income and plan on transferring their wealth to their children and grandchildren. They have three children, all of whom are married and have two children. The three children plus three spouses plus six more children make a total of twelve family members. Because both the husband and wife can each give $11,000 to each family member, potentially they can give $132,000 ($11,000 x 12 each). Combined, they can give $264,000 every year to their family—$11,000 from each parent to each child, spouse, and grandchild.

Remember that the three-year time limit must be satisfied for gifts to be excluded from your estate. This technique can save a very significant amount of estate taxes. I can't estimate specifically how much it saves for you because it depends on how long you live, how long you give, and the number of people you give to. You can leverage this idea even further.

4. *Give away assets that will likely appreciate rapidly in value to reduce the future potential value of your estate.* This idea is essentially a turbo-charged version of item 3 above. Instead of giving cash each year, you could give shares of stock or land that may increase in value in the future. By doing so, you eliminate future growth of your estate and limit estate taxes.

Let's say that in 1988 you bought six hundred shares of a growing software company for $30,000. The stock began to increase, and you believed that one day this relatively small software company could dominate the technology world. You gave 150 shares to each of your four children at Christmas 1988. Based on the value of the stock at Christmas, you gave each of them a gift that was valued at $9,000— less than the annual gift exclusion. Therefore, no taxation resulted at the time of the gift, and no usage of your unified credit occurred.

Your children held on to the shares of that company, which later did dominate the technology world. If you had held on to the stock within your estate, then all of the increase would be subject to estate tax. But giving away the stock before it appreciated allowed you to leverage your tax-free wealth transfer. The potential tax savings could range from a few thousand to theoretically a few million dollars given the right circumstances.

If you own assets that have already appreciated substantially, then it may be wiser to hold these or use a more advanced technique. My standard advice is to work with a certified public accountant and/or your lawyer to understand the potential income tax and estate tax impact of giving business or investment property.

5. *Use an irrevocable life insurance trust (ILIT) to exclude life insur-*

ance proceeds from your estate. With a wee bit of legal work, setting up an ILIT can save a very significant amount of estate taxes. In simplified terms, here's how this idea works.

The ILIT, that is the trust, owns the insurance policy. You are the insured. When you set up the ILIT, you name the beneficiaries of it. You also name the trustee of the ILIT. You pay the premiums each year; this action is considered a contribution to the trust. The trustee makes sure the premiums are paid, receives notices, notifies the insurance company upon your death, and basically has the power to act on behalf of the trust.

In essence, you have given up ownership of the policy in exchange for getting proceeds to beneficiaries of your choice. Because life insurance proceeds are not taxable for income taxes, your beneficiaries receive the full value of the insurance death benefit. No estate taxes are subtracted and no income taxes are subtracted.

Just one of these ideas is well worth the price of this book! Perhaps you may apply one or more of them if they make sense for your facts and circumstances. Once again, check with your professional legal and tax advisers to ensure compliance with current tax provisions and avoid any other problems or challenges with your situation. See appendix B for more information about the Christian Financial Professionals Network (www.cfpn.org).

Conclusion

When establishing your estate plan, you need to pay particular attention to the titling of assets, such as property and brokerage accounts, and the beneficiary designations of life insurance contracts and retirement plans. The titling of assets and beneficiary designations will override the guidelines of a will in many cases.

There are many other technical aspects of estate planning that are beyond the scope of this book. Revocable living trusts, charitable remainder and charitable lead trusts, charitable gift annuities, grantor trusts, irrevocable life insurance trusts, as well as different methods of property ownership are all vehicles and techniques that could enhance an overall estate plan. The use of these will depend upon your goals and the makeup and size of your estate and will require the input of a qualified professional.

Estate planning is an integral part of financial planning, but it is not financial planning in its entirety. Both financial planning and estate planning need to begin at an early age. They are dynamic in nature, and to procrastinate in either area is poor stewardship.

15

GIVING LIVING

*"If you want to be rich, give; if you want to be poor, grasp;
if you want abundance, scatter; if you want to be needy, hoard!"*
UNKNOWN

*"What I kept I lost.
What I spent I had.
What I gave I have."*
PERSIAN PROVERB

*"The world will never be won to Christ with what
people can conveniently spare."*
BERNARD EDINGER

"It is more blessed to give than receive."
ACTS 20:35B

Several years ago a speaker at a missions conference in my church quoted the statistics that show more money is spent on both chewing gum and dog food in the United States than is given to foreign missions. I cannot vouch for the accuracy of these numbers, nor am I saying you should never chew gum or feed your pet. I am saying the IRS reports that Americans, on the average, give less than 1.7 percent of their adjusted gross income for charitable contributions. That should change.

As a financial planner, my first paying client was a man who said his goal for the rest of his life was to retire as soon as possible in order to work full-time on the mission field. In addition, he wanted to maintain his present lifestyle and continue to give at the 15 percent level as he was then doing. He was a fifty-two-year-old physician with two children who were both grown and educated. He had a net worth of around $350,000, and his income was approximately $85,000 per year. I asked him and his wife to share with me any dreams they might have for their lives. They both agreed that one of their desires was to give $1,000,000 to the Lord's work before they died. I thought to myself that this was obviously impossible with their income and net worth.

However, about sixty days later, after their financial plan was prepared, I called him and said, "Doc, I hope you're sitting down, because I have some shocking news for you. First of all, how would you like to retire in five years and have approximately $1,000,000 in investments at that time?" He thought that sounded like a great idea, and then I told him that, according to our projections, it was also possible for them to give away $1,000,000 during that same five-year time period. To say the least, he was shocked and frankly disbelieving.

I met with him and his wife to go over their plan and showed them that they, in fact, had a much higher net worth than they originally thought because of the escalation in value of some of the real estate they owned. By taking a long-range perspective on their planning, it was possible for them to begin giving away some of their assets while they were, at the same time, replacing them out of their current cash flow. Finally, I told them that all of this was possible for two reasons: first of all, because of their desire to give, and second, because they had lived and were continuing to live a nonconsumptive lifestyle.

It has now been several years since we prepared their plan. Even though it did not work out exactly as projected, they have been fairly well able to accomplish the objectives they originally gave me . . . because God always has creative alternatives.

I have been able to share the same principles that I learned from this couple with others, and we have seen many clients make a commitment to give substantial sums of money. From my observations I think there are three reasons why Christians who desire to give, don't give more.

First of all, they don't know that they can give and still meet the other goals and objectives they have. They have never really analyzed their financial resources to know what obligations and opportunities they have. It's very difficult to be a good steward when you don't know what you have.

Second, they don't know how to give. They are not aware of all the various ways to give. In the doctor's case mentioned above, one of the techniques that we used was to give away property that had appreciated in value, thereby avoiding the capital gains tax on it. Furthermore, he still got a deduction for the full fair market value of the property. Through the use of this technique, he was able to reduce his taxes to a very low amount, which freed up cash to be invested in replacement of the property that had been given. It still cost him to do the giving, but it cost him less to give this way than if he had given cash.

The third and most important reason that people don't give is that they don't *plan* to give. It is the same issue that we have been dealing with throughout this book: We live a life of being a responder rather than a planner. It has been my experience that, with planning, giving for a family goes up, on average, about five times what they were giving prior to doing planning. A very well-known and wealthy American told me one time, "Any man, and especially a businessman, has more uses for money than the money available. Therefore, unless he plans to give, he never will give." A person whose lifestyle is consumptive can never accumulate enough to be able to give substantial amounts of money away. Giving is never a cause of spiritual growth—it is rather a function of spiritual growth.

Biblical Answers to the Questions of Giving

There are three very relevant questions to ask yourself as you plan to give:

1. When should I give?

2. Where should I give?

3. How much should I give?

As a result of reviewing guidelines and principles in Scripture, I believe there are six words that answer the questions of when to give, where to give, and how much to give:

When?	*Where?*	*How much?*
❖ Preemptively	❖ Purposefully	❖ Proportionately
❖ Periodically		❖ Planned
		❖ Precommitted

When to Give

Preemptive giving is clearly defined in Proverbs 3:9: "Honor the LORD with your possessions, and with the first fruits of all your increase." To me, this means that giving to God's work should have the first priority over all other uses of money, and therefore I give, preempting all other uses, until I have met that commitment.

"On the first day of the week let each one of you lay something aside, storing up as he may prosper, that there be no collections when I come" (1 Corinthians 16:2). Not only should I give preemptively, but I should also give periodically. To take this Scripture literally would be to say that, on each Sunday of the week, some amount should be put aside and saved for giving purposes. So the "when" question is answered—giving should be the first priority use of the income, and this giving should be done as it is received, that is, on a periodic basis.

Where to Give

When answering the question, where should I give? we should make a purposeful decision to give where the Scripture says God's interest is. "For the administration of this service not only supplies the needs of the saints, but also is abounding through many thanksgivings to God" (2 Corinthians 9:12).

God definitely commands us to meet the needs of the saints and to fulfill the Great Commission. Thus, our purposes in giving are to give for the needy, for evangelism, and for discipleship in *our* Judea, *our* Samaria, and to the uttermost parts of the earth (Acts 1:8). Giving must be taken very seriously and decided upon consciously in order to fulfill the commands of Scripture.

To help answer the question, where should I give? we can build a matrix. Down one side are the biblical admonitions to give to evangelism, discipleship, the poor, the widows, the orphans, and the needy. Across the top of the chart are the locations—Judea, Samaria, and the uttermost parts of the earth—or in our contemporary situations, my city, my state, my country, and the rest of the world.

As you review chart 15-A, write in the giving that you are now doing. You will be able to see how well you are fulfilling the biblical admonitions in terms of places and needs. Giving to your local church should be the best place to give to meet the needs of the saints and for evangelism of the lost—assuming your church follows biblical teaching. In other words, you may meet all these needs by giving to your local church. You may also wish to give to other ministries or organizations that address these admonitions. You then need to ask the question, am I giving all that I should be giving?

How Much to Give

How much to give in quantitative terms is not as important as our attitude toward giving. In 2 Corinthians 9:7, we read that our giving should be done "not grudgingly or of necessity; for God loves a cheerful giver." In 2 Corinthians 8:9, Paul gave us the example of Christ to suggest the right attitude toward giving: "For you know the grace of our Lord Jesus Christ, that though He was rich, yet for your sakes He became poor, that you through His poverty might become rich." So, the attitude of giving must be one of cheerfulness and grace. Freely we have received; freely we must give.

The question, how much should I give? is not a simple matter. "For I testify that they gave as much as they were able, and even beyond their ability. Entirely on their own, they urgently pleaded with us for the privilege of sharing in this service to the saints. And they did not do as we expected but they gave themselves first to the Lord and then to us in keeping with God's will" (2 Corinthians 8:3–5).

Therefore, we are not limited in how much we give either by what we can see or according to our abilities, but what God instructs us each to do. That will vary for each Christian family.

Through consideration of the three P's we have mentioned, we can come to a right answer of how much: We should give *proportionately* on a *planned* basis and on a *precommited* basis. Give an amount that is proportionate to the amount that God has prospered you. You should, by planning, give more than a proportionate amount, and you should commit in advance to give some of the amount God provides on a totally unexpected basis; for example, a bonus, an inheritance, or a gift.

Giving Plan

Chart 15-A

CAUSE	MY CITY	MY STATE	MY COUNTRY	WORLD	HOW MUCH (1)
Evangelism					
Discipleship					
Poor					
Widows					
Orphans					
				TOTAL $	

(1) How much:
    Proportionally—should   _____
    Planned—could   _____
    Precommitted—would   _____
    TOTAL $_____

When:
    As received—Preemptively
                —Periodically

Application

These principles work themselves out in three levels of giving—the "should give" level, the "could give" level, and the "would give" level. The "should give" level includes our proportionate giving. Each Christian should give in proportion to the amount that he or she has received. The Bible instructs that the starting point is 10 percent of our gross income.

The "could give" level is the amount that I could give if I were willing to give up something else. It may mean that I give up a vacation, a savings account, a lifestyle desire, or something else. Giving at this level is the closest any American Christian can come to sacrificial giving as described in Luke 21:4: "For all these out of their abundance have put in offerings for God, but she out of her poverty has put in all the livelihood that she had." Sacrificial giving is giving up something in order to give to the Lord. I recommend that after a financial plan is put together a family should regularly choose to give up something in order to give at the "could give" level. This level requires no faith, so it is not a faith pledge. There is no faith required because you can see the amount, and faith, by definition, requires seeing the unseen. It is simply a sacrificial love gift, an exercise to tangibly show God your love, your willingness to trust Him, and your loose hold on the things and desires of earth.

The third level of giving more clearly approximates faith giving, and I call it precommitted giving (committing in advance), or the "would give" level. We commit ourselves to giving if God provides a certain amount supernaturally. God can do this only if there is a financial plan in place that allows us to see His providing an additional cash-flow margin through either additional income or decreased expenses. Unless we are precommitted to give the additional surplus, we will not give it, and we may miss out on having the incredible blessing of seeing His hand at work to provide in unique ways.

In summary, how much we can give is dependent upon three levels: I should give an amount proportionate to my income; I could give an additional amount by giving up something; and I would give more if God increased my cash-flow margin. The how much is not dependent upon a set formula, and it gives us the opportunity to see God at work in our financial lives.

Many times I am asked whether one should give now or should build an investment base in order to be able to give later. In our earlier illustrations, we saw that $10,000 compounding at 25 percent over forty years grows to $75,231,000. Wouldn't a person do better to find an investment at 25 percent to compound it and then give the $75,231,000 rather than the mere $10,000?

The way I answer this question is with another question: Is God limited to 25 percent compounding? Even though there is no biblical interest rate stated, the Bible does point out in many places that he who sows sparingly shall also reap sparingly, and that God causes fruit to grow at thirty-fold, sixty-fold, and one hundred-fold. In percentage terms, thirty-fold is 3,000 percent; sixty-fold is 6,000 percent; and one hundred-fold is 10,000 percent. I don't believe it is wrong to assume that God's rate of compounding is 3,000 percent, 6,000 percent, 10,000 percent, and even greater.

Then I would ask the question, is an investment of $10,000, compounding at 25 percent, comparable to giving the amount of $10,000, compounding at 10,000 percent, for all eternity? That is the real comparison. Matthew 6:19–24 makes clear that our treasure will either be on earth ($75,231,000) or in heaven ($10,000 x 10,000 percent x eternity). Without question, the eternal perspective on giving makes the temporal perspective of no consequence. Remember: He owns it all and knows the earthly interest rates. If He is prompting you to give now, do so without hesitation, regardless of the what-ifs down the road. He is Lord over the what-ifs—both on a personal and worldwide level.

As someone once said to me, "Do your giving while you're living so you're knowing where it's going." And the martyred missionary Jim Elliot said, "He is no fool who gives up what he cannot keep in order to gain what he cannot lose." Whether to give now or later is really a silly question when you put it into the perspective of the Almighty.

God is perfectly able to handle your investment of His resources in His kingdom and to cause it to grow and to compound at the greatest rate. He does not need your expertise or skill to cause an investment to grow in order to be able to give more later.

Faith Giving Pledge

Chart 15-B

Recognizing that God wants us to be good stewards of His resources and use them for His purposes, we make the following giving pledge for the coming year:

AMOUNT

What we ***should*** give:

What we ***could*** give by making a sacrifice in the following area:

What we ***would*** give if God blesses us with:

WE WILL GIVE $

Sign Name

Sign Name

Chart 15-B gives you an opportunity to make a faith giving pledge for the coming year. It breaks the faith giving pledge down to the three levels of giving—what you should give, what you could give, and what you would give. You cannot complete this pledge until:

1. You have summarized your financial situation and determined what amount of proportionate giving you are going to do.

2. You know what amount of sacrificial giving you are going to do by giving up something.

3. You know what your cash-flow margin is—that which you would give if God caused it to be more than you anticipated.

My challenge for you is to prayerfully make the pledge and then watch what God does to cause it to become a reality!

Don't Miss the Miracle

I have often wondered what it is going to be like to stand before the Lord and have Him evaluate my works. I wonder whether I will hear Him say, "Well done, good and faithful servant; you were faithful over a few things, I will make you ruler over many things. Enter into the joy of your lord" (Matthew 25:21). Or, on the other hand, will I watch as most of the works that I have accomplished are consumed by fire? My greatest fear is that I may fervently work at the wrong task rather than faithfully complete God's work for me.

Mark 6:30–44 is a passage on which I often reflect.

Then the apostles gathered to Jesus and told Him all things, both what they had done and what they had taught. And He said to them, "Come aside by yourselves to a deserted place and rest a while." For there were many coming and going, and they did not even have time to eat. So they departed to a deserted place in the boat by themselves.

But the multitudes saw them departing, and many knew Him and ran there on foot from all the cities. They arrived before them and came together to Him. And Jesus, when He came out, saw a great multitude and was moved with compassion for them, because they were like sheep not having a shepherd. So He began to teach them many things. When the day was now far spent, His disciples came to Him and said, "This is a deserted place, and already the hour is late. Send them away, that they may go into the surrounding country and villages and buy themselves bread; for they have nothing to eat."

But He answered and said to them, "You give them something to eat." And they said to Him, "Shall we go and buy two hundred denarii worth of bread and give them something to eat?" But He said to them, "How many loaves do you have? Go and see." And when they found out they said, "Five, and two fish."

Then He commanded them to make them all sit down in groups on the green grass. So they sat down in ranks, in hundreds and in fifties.

And when He had taken the five loaves and the two fish, He looked up to heaven, blessed and broke the loaves, and gave them to His disciples to set before them; and the two fish He divided among them all. So they all ate and were filled. And they took up twelve baskets full of fragments and of the fish. Now those who had eaten the loaves were about five thousand men.

Many conclusions that are applicable to financial planning can be drawn from this passage because financial planning is, in reality, the working out of your life priorities. Let's examine the principles I have gleaned from this passage.

Principle 1—Spend time with God to know His wisdom.

Jesus said, "Come aside by yourselves to a deserted place and rest a while" (Mark 6:31). The first step to financial planning is to be alone with God and listen to what He has to say. It is not the development of a plan, it is not getting advice, but it is spending time alone with Him.

Unless you hear God's voice, you cannot take a second step. Jesus recognized this principle, and it is obvious in His life because He spent much time alone with God prior to making any major decision. Can we do less?

Principle 2—Don't be married to your plan.

"Jesus, when He came out, saw a great multitude and was moved with compassion for them, because they were like sheep not having a shepherd. So He began to teach them many things" (Mark 6:34). A second principle is that our plan should not be our god. Jesus had a plan to go with His disciples to a quiet place; however, when He saw the needs, He had compassion on the people and was responsive to God's direction in His life at that point. To be totally committed to a plan is to make a serious mistake. God works in our lives through many circumstances, and to ignore them because of a plan is to run the risk of missing God's will. Changing a plan doesn't mean you misheard or that God changed His mind. It just means that His plan and direction may differ from your timing.

Principle 3—Seek the mind of Christ, not the mind of man.

"His disciples came to Him and said, 'This is a deserted place, and already the hour is late. Send them away, that they may go into the surrounding country and villages and buy themselves bread'" (Mark 6:35–36). I have often asked myself, "What's wrong with this advice?" The answer is, nothing—except that it was wrong. It was very practical and logical, but it was not in accordance with what Jesus intended at that point. Don't ever thwart God because of merely a practical consideration. God wants to do things in His way, in His time. Practicality does not always coincide with faith. It is not wrong in itself; it simply could be wrong in light of what God wants to accomplish.

Although worldly advice can be logical, its source is not based on God's truth. Many Christians fall into the trap of listening to non-Christian counselors and expect the non-Christian counselor to give them godly advice. The advice may sound good and may even be good, but unless it is advice that comes from God, it is wrong.

Principle 4—Obedience is critical to success.

The disciples argued a bit with Jesus regarding His plan, but Jesus did not argue back. Finally He directed them to have all the people sit down on the grass. This was very illogical because, at that point, they did not have the food to feed them. But the disciples—and the people—obeyed. If God says to do it, I do it. If God says to give, I give. If God says to pay off debt—I do it. If God says to pay my taxes, I do so. If God says to increase or decrease my lifestyle, I do so. The issue is obedience.

Principle 5—Financial plans are faith plans.

When the disciples had the people sit down on the grass, there were three elements present that are always present in a faith plan. First of all, they obviously could not see how the people were going to be fed. Oftentimes, in a financial plan, we may not see how our goal is going to be accomplished either. Second, inadequate resources were available or owned by the disciples to accomplish the goal of feeding them. That may be characteristic of our financial plan, that we have inadequate resources. Third, the disciples did not know what the next step was going to be to fulfill God's plan. Thus, a faith plan for us may require action without our full understanding. I think of Noah's building an ark for 120 years, not fully understanding what God was going to do; or Abraham's leaving Ur, not knowing where God was leading him.

Principle 6—Don't miss the miracle!

Mark 6:42–43 says, "They all ate and were filled. And they took up twelve baskets full of fragments and of the fish." The results of operating according to a faith plan are that the goal will be reached, God will be glorified, and growth will occur. In the case of the feeding of five thousand, the goal was reached, the Lord received the glory, and the disciples should have experienced growth in their faith.

However, if you read on in the passage, you come down to verses 51–52, "Then He went up into the boat to them, and the wind ceased. And they were greatly amazed in themselves beyond measure, and marveled. For they had not understood about the loaves, because their heart was hardened." What a tragedy! Just a few hours earlier they had seen an unbelievable miracle. As a matter of fact, they had participated in the miracle by handing out the bread and fish, and then gathering up the twelve baskets. However, the Scripture says, "They were greatly amazed in themselves beyond measure, and marveled. For they had not understood about the loaves, because their heart was hardened."

The challenge is, don't plan God out of your finances. Don't have a closed mind. Don't miss the miracle. I hope that much has been given to you in this book that is practical and useful; but don't miss the miracle of what God wants to do in your life by saying, "It is not appropriate or applicable in my situation, for surely God could not want to do that for me."

God merely wants you to take the first step, then the second step, then the third step, so that when you stand before Him, you will finally understand that whatever has been accomplished has been accomplished by Him. Because of your faithfulness with regard to what He has given you, you will hear Him say, "Well done, good and faithful servant; you were faithful over a few things, I will make you ruler over many things. Enter into the joy of your lord" (Matthew 25:21).

Appendix A

How a Family Conference Can Help Your Finances

Here's a provocative question: *Is it easier to train your children in financial principles around the coffee table or from your coffin?* Obviously the correct answer is the first one. But why do so many parents wait until it's too late?

Perhaps you are the one parent in a thousand who can easily discuss and develop financial plans with your children. But if not, the family conference can provide tremendous benefits as well as peace of mind.

There are two *general* purposes for family conferences. First and foremost, it is an opportunity for communication among family members regarding finances. As parents, we are responsible for training our children in all areas of life, including the financial area. The family conference offers parents the opportunity to communicate their philosophy, beliefs, and values regarding finances to their children, as well to communicate financial decisions that will affect the children. Although the parents have a right to do with their assets as they desire, the family conference will allow for dialogue concerning important issues while all parties are present, rather than after a death (which, by the way, is usually when a "family conference" occurs).

Because of this healthy communication, the family conference will enhance family harmony. Money can cause tremendous conflict without the family members being aware of it. Communicating about money promotes harmony and often avoids the bitterness that may be generated over money decisions.

The second general purpose for the family conference is for child training. It is an opportunity for Mom and Dad to begin to teach their children about budgeting, investment planning, estate planning, and other financial responsibilities. Children can see their parents implementing and modeling wise financial stewardship. As they see their parents plan, they are more likely to plan in the future as well.

Not only are family conferences productive in a general sense, but they are usually beneficial in the following *specific* situations.

First, family conferences are usually conducted concerning estate planning. Mom and Dad can explain to their children their current estate plan and why they have set it up that way. Together the family can discuss amounts to be given to charity and even select the specific charities. Reasons for equal and unequal distribution to the children can be explained. The children can be honest about their feelings regarding the amounts their parents are leaving to them. Many Christians may improperly believe that just because they have children, their estate should go to them. Yet the scriptural precedent is that the money should be left to those who have demonstrated sound stewardship. According to Ecclesiastes 7:11–12, if we leave money to someone to whom we have not left wisdom, it can be a devastating situation. Therefore, in many cases discussing estate planning can be a catalyst to help children get "on board" financially and become fiscally responsible.

A second specific purpose for family conferences is to discuss current giving. Parents should be careful that they are not unduly restricting their children while at the same time giving huge sums of money to charity. Right or wrong, it is easy to cause bitterness and drive a wedge between a parent and child if the child sees the parent giving a lot of money to charity but then withholding things from him. Those choices are the parents' responsibility; however, communicating with the children will help them understand your motivation and expectations for them and alleviate the potential bitterness and disharmony.

A third reason for the family conference is to explain to children the benefits of budgeting. Helping your children establish a simple budget can be a major step to lifelong fiscal responsibility.

The most effective family conferences involve a facilitator (such as a financial planner or attorney) who directs and mediates the discussion. Mom, Dad, the children, and their spouses (if appropriate) are present. Other advisors (an insurance agent or accountant, for example) may also be present if decisions involving them will take place. However, a family conference may simply involve the parents sitting down with their children and explaining what they are doing financially and why. The timing of the conference depends on the specific goal to be discussed. You could wait until your children are in their teens before involving them in the estate or giving conferences, or budgeting conferences could begin at an earlier age.

Appendix B

The Christian Financial Professionals Network

(Ron to insert info about CFPN)

Glossary

After-Tax Return—The yield of an investment after taxes have been taken out.

Annuity (Immediate)—An individual pays an insurance company a specified capital sum in exchange for a promise that the insurer will, at some time in the future, begin to make a series of periodic payments to the individual for as long as he/she lives or for some other specified period of time.

Appreciation—An increase in fair market value.

Assets—Everything a person owns, including cash, investments, house, or autos. It includes physical, tangible assets as well as intangible assets.

Balance Sheet—A condensed financial statement showing the amount and nature of an individual's assets and liabilities at a given time. A "snapshot" of what a person owns and what he owes. Sometimes referred to as a net worth statement.

Basis—The price paid for an asset. Used to figure capital gains tax.

Beneficiary—One who is designated to receive a benefit; for example, the person who would receive the proceeds of a life insurance settlement.

Bid and Asked—The "bid" is the highest price anyone is willing to pay for a security at a given time; the "asked" is the lowest price anyone will take at that time. Stocks are usually purchased at "bid" and sold at "asked."

Bond—A promise of a corporation, municipality, government, church, etc., to pay interest at a stated rate and repay face value of the bond. It is a loan from you to the organization to mature at a specified date.

Budget—A plan or guideline for spending.

Capital Gain—Profit or loss from the sale of a capital asset such as real estate, stock, commercial property, land, equipment, etc. Any capital asset held at least one year is classified as long-term and receives favorable income tax treatment.

Capital Needs—In personal financial planning, the amount of capital (assets or cash) needed in a lump sum to enable one to meet income needs and expenses should death or disability occur.

Cash Flow—The process of money coming in from various sources (income) and being spent on various uses (expenses). A cash-flow statement is a look at both the income and the expenses over any period of time, but is usually for at least a month and/or for a year.

Cash Surrender Value—The actual value of your life insurance policy. It is the amount of cash you would receive if you voluntarily terminate your policy before it matures. It is also the amount that can be borrowed from your policy while still keeping the policy in force. This value can be found in the policy contract. It may be more than the contract value, as it can be increased by dividends and interest on dividends, which are left to accumulate (dividend deposits).

Common Stock—Securities that represent an ownership interest in a corporation. They generally have dividend and appreciation potential.

Cost Per Thousand—Refers to the cost of each thousand dollars of life insurance protection.

Current Assets—Those assets that can easily be converted into cash or sold in a short period of time. Example: stocks, certificates of deposit, cash value of life insurance, money market funds, etc. Also known as liquid assets.

Debt—A sum owed to someone else, either a financial or personal obligation; a state of owing.

DIVERSIFICATION—Spreading money among different types of investments.

DIVIDENDS—The payment designated by a corporation to be distributed pro-rata among outstanding shares of stock. Corporations usually declare dividends from their profits, and the amount is in relation to the amount of the profit.

DIVIDEND ELECTION—The method you choose to receive your dividends. Most commonly refers to life insurance. You may elect dividends to be paid in cash, to reduce premiums, to buy paid-up additions, or to accumulate at interest.

DOLLAR COST AVERAGING—A method of purchasing securities at regular intervals with a fixed amount of dollars, regardless of the prevailing prices of the securities. Payments buy more shares when the price is low and fewer shares when it rises. Because of the fluctuations of the market, this method enables an investor who consistently buys in both good and bad times to be able to improve his potential for a gain when he sells. It is an effective method for a single investor to strategically invest his money.

EFFECTIVE RATE—The amount of each dollar earned which goes to pay taxes. The ratio of total taxes paid to gross income.

FACE VALUE—The amount the insurance company promises to pay at death of insured.

FIDUCIARY—One who acts for another in financial matters.

FIXED—Refers to an asset in which principal does not grow in value. You will never get back more or less than you invested if held to maturity. Example: certificates of deposit, cash value, bonds, etc. These assets are fixed yield in nature.

INDIVIDUAL RETIREMENT ACCOUNT (IRA)—A retirement provision established by law, which allows an individual to set aside funds for future retirement and receive tax advantages. A traditional IRA provides an immediate tax deduction and grows tax-deferred. Taxes are paid when the traditional IRA is distributed. A Roth IRA provides no immediate tax deduction, but all the growth in value is tax free. There are no taxes when the Roth IRA is distributed.

INFLATION—An increase in the volume of money and credit relative to available goods resulting in a substantial and continuing rise in the general price level.

INFLATIONARY SPIRAL—A continuous rise in prices that is sustained by the interaction of usage increases and cost increases.

INVESTMENT—The use of money for the purpose of making more money: to gain income, increase capital, save taxes, or a combination of the three.

KEOGH OR SMALL BUSINESS RETIREMENT PLAN—Similar to an IRA, but designed for small businesses or self-employed individuals. These small business plans (sometimes called SIMPLE Profit Sharing, or Simplified Employee Pension [SEP] plans), permit the setting aside of a specified part of current earnings for use as a retirement fund in the future. The amount deductible for these plans may be much greater than the limits on IRAs or 401(k)s.

LEVERAGE—The use of a small amount of equity or assets to control or purchase an asset worth substantially more. The value to the investor is that you receive appreciation on the total worth of the asset, not just your equity. Although leveraging increases your earnings potential, one is "at risk" for the amount leveraged (the loan). Example: If you put $10,000 down and borrow $70,000 to buy an $80,000 home, you have leveraged.

LIABILITIES—All the claims against you. Obligations you owe. Some may be current (owed within the year), such as credit card loans; others may be long term, such as a home mortgage.

LIQUIDITY (LIQUID)—The state of assets readily converted to cash at their current fair market value. A liquid asset will not lose value upon its sale as a result of a lack of a ready market.

LONG-TERM ASSETS (NONLIQUID)—Those assets that cannot easily be converted to cash or sold or consumed in a short period of time. Example: home, real estate, land assets, etc.

MARGIN—In this book, margin means the cash sources less the cash uses. The amount you have left to spend as you desire after all living expenses, mandatory commitments, and taxes are met. (Margin has another meaning in the context of stock brokerage accounts: borrowing funds from your broker to purchase financial securities.)

MARGINAL RATE—The tax bracket percentage from which your income tax is calculated. For example, in the case of a person in the 28 percent tax bracket, twenty-eight cents of each additional dollar earned would go to the government in taxes.

MARITAL DEDUCTION—In calculating estate tax, a deduction allowed by law against the estate of the first spouse to die. The amount of the qualifying property or deduction is the entire estate of the first to die.

MINIMUM DEPOSIT—When the cash-value increases in the insurance policy are used to pay the premiums of the policy.

MONEY MARKET FUND—A mutual fund that invests in money market instruments such as treasury bills, U.S. government agency issues, commercial bank certificates of deposit, commercial paper, etc. The interest rate on a money market fund fluctuates with the prime interest rate.

MORTGAGE—Usually refers to the balance of the loan on a home. The amount of money borrowed to purchase a home.

NONLIQUID—Investments not easily converted to cash at their current fair market value.

PREFERRED STOCK—Similar to common stock. Generally less dividend and appreciation potential but receives a higher priority or preference over common stock in dividend payments or in the event of liquidation.

PREMIUM—The payment an insurance policy holder agrees to make for coverage.

PRESENT VALUE—The value of a sum of money to be received in the future in today's dollars, taking into account either interest rates, inflation, or both. (Example: $10,000 received in 2015 may have a present value of $6,830.)

PRIME RATE—The interest rate charged by large U.S. money-center commercial banks to their best business borrowers.

PRINCIPAL—A person's capital or money. Used for investments. Sometimes referred to as equity when talking about a house.

PROSPECTUS—A circular that describes securities or investments being offered for sale to the public.

PURCHASING POWER—The ability of a dollar to buy a product or service. As prices increase, purchasing power decreases. Today's dollar will not buy as much today as it would in 1980.

UNIFIED CREDIT—A credit, established by law, applied to tentative federal estate taxes owed upon death of an individual. It is like an exemption amount for estate taxes.

VARIABLE—Refers to assets which have the potential to grow; primarily concerned with appreciation. Examples: stocks, real estate, etc. These may be sold for more or less than you invested.

WILL—The directions of a testator (the male or female who makes the will) regarding the final disposition of his or her estate.

WITHHOLDING—Refers to the amount of tax withheld from a paycheck.

WITHHOLDING ALLOWANCES—Used by an employer to calculate the amount withheld monthly from your check for federal and state taxes.

YIELD—Dividends or interest paid by a company expressed as a percentage of current selling price.

AUTHOR INFORMATION

Ron Blue is president of Christian Financial Planning Institute. Following his graduation from Indiana University with a Masters of Business Administration degree, Ron joined the management group of Peat, Marwick, Mitchell & Co. and worked with the firm in New York, Dallas, and San Francisco.

In 1970, Ron founded an Indianapolis-based CPA firm that has grown to be one of the fifty largest CPA firms in the United States. Leaving the firm in 1977, Ron became administrative vice president of Leadership Dynamics International. While with Leadership Dynamics, he was involved in developing and teaching biblically based leadership and management seminars in the United States and Africa.

Convinced that Christians would better handle their personal finances if they were counseled objectively with the highest technical expertise and from a biblical perspective, he founded a financial planning firm in 1979. That firm grew to manage over $2.5 billion in assets for its more than 5,000 clients nationwide with a staff of more than 175 people in fourteen regional offices.

Ron retired from Ronald Blue & Co. in 2003 in order to lead an international effort to equip and motivate Christian financial professionals to serve the body of Christ by implementing biblical wisdom in their lives and practices. This venture has resulted in financial freedom and increased giving by multiplied thousands of Christians.

Ron is the author of nine books on personal finance from a biblical perspective. He is featured in the popular six-part Master Your Money video series, produced by Walk Thru the Bible Ministries and used in more than 5,500 churches across the country.

Ron has appeared on numerous radio and television programs, including *Focus on the Family, Family News in Focus, The 700 Club, Prime Time America,* and *Moody Radio Open Line.* He is a regular contributor to several national Christian magazines.

Ron currently serves on the boards of directors of Campus Crusade for Christ, Crown Financial Ministries, the National Christian Foundation, and Thomas Nelson, Inc., a New York Stock Exchange listed company. He also serves on the boards of trustees of the Maclellan Foundation and the Sandra and William B. Johnson Foundation,

Inc. He formerly served on the boards of directors of Family Research Council, Promise Keepers, Insight for Living, the Medical Institute, and Walk Thru the Bible Ministries.

In 2002, Ron received the Honors Award from the Georgia chapter of the Financial Planning Association (FPA). In 2003, he received the honored designation of Distinguished Entrepreneur from the Indiana University Kelley School of Business, his alma mater.

Ron and Judy live in Atlanta. They have five children and six grandchildren.

Jeremy L. White has been a Certified Public Accountant for sixteen years with financial experience in public accounting and industry. His CPA firm specializes in personal financial services, such as tax preparation, financial counseling, wealth transfer planning, and retirement planning.

Jeremy has previously assisted with several national best-selling financial books including writing with Ron Blue *Splitting Heirs: Giving Your Money and Things to Your Children Without Ruining Their Lives.* Jeremy also wrote with Ron Blue and the late Larry Burkett the best-selling book *Wealth to Last: Money Essentials for the Second Half of Life.*

Jeremy has been a contributor for five years to Larry Burkett's *Money Matters* newsletter. He also assisted Larry Burkett and Crown Financial Ministries as the primary writing consultant in updating their successful workbook *Family Financial Planning.* He has been a frequent guest on Crown Financial Ministries' *How to Manage Your Money* radio broadcast.

Before founding his own financial firm, Jeremy worked with the national accounting firm of Ernst & Young in their Miami, Florida, office. Jeremy's firm provides tax preparation, small business advisory services, estate planning, and financial seminars. His office can be reached at 1-888-296-5616. For free tax tips and an archive of articles, see his website at www.consultcpa.com. He is a member of the Christian Financial Professionals Network.

Jeremy and his wife, Sharon, live in Paducah, Kentucky, where they homeschool their two daughters, Jenaye and Jaclyn.